The Middle School Maze

The MiDDLe ScHooL Maze

CLiFF SchimmeLS

ChariotVICTOR
PUBLISHING
A DIVISION OF COOK COMMUNICATIONS

Editor: Afton Rorvik
Designer and Typesetter: Andrea Boven
Cartoons: John Duckworth
Production: Julianne Marotz

Library of Congress Cataloging-in-Publication Data

Schimmels, Cliff.
    The middle school maze / Cliff Schimmels.
        p. cm.
    ISBN 1-56476-431-1
        1. Parent and teenager—United States. 2. Teenagers—United States.
3. Middle school students—United States. 4. Adolescent psychology—United
States. 5. Parenting—United States. I. Title.
HQ799.15.S33 1996
649'.125—dc20   96-24413
                                                                    CIP

---

1 2 3 4 5 6 7 8 9 10 Printing/Year 00 99 98 97 96

Dedication

to Alyssa, Ann, Delaney, and Will

for calling me by the

highest title available

to mortal males—

Grandpa!

Contents

"Another junior high flashback, Dear?"

Introduction

Not long ago I attended one of those after-church Sunday evening parties. The wassail was warm and the mood was light. Our little group started telling funny stories about growing up, and we celebrated those stories with joy and laughter.

I decided to use that pleasant climate to do a bit of research; so I said, "I'll tell you what let's do. Let's all tell a funny story about being in junior high."

Silence! All over the room, silence! People stared at their feet with strained expressions on their faces.

I realized that I had made the test too hard, so I modified the assignment. "Let's just tell any story about junior high, funny or not."

More silence! Without saying a word, without smiling, people began to get up, put on their coats, and leave.

The hostess still hasn't forgiven me for breaking up her party, but I did come to a sobering conclusion.

Most of us had such a miserable time during our junior high years that we have blocked the whole experience out of our memories. The pain was so great that we have no recollection of our behavior or emotions. Now that we have children or grandchildren or neighbors going through those very same experiences, we can't identify. We just know that we didn't act that way. These are surely the strangest animals we have ever seen, and we don't understand them at all.

This is the paradox. At a time when our children need us the most, we aren't much help.

Every day I hear the sad pleas.

"I don't know what happened to him. He used to be such a nice guy and now all he wants to do is sleep and argue."

"She was such a nice little girl, and we were so close. But now that she has turned thirteen it seems that we are mortal enemies."

"If I could just know what he is thinking. What's going on in his mind?"

I have a confession. I like these people. At times I don't understand them either, but I like them. That's why I've chosen to spend my life among them. For fifteen years, I taught them in the classrooms, coached their sports teams, directed their plays, and watched them grow. For the last twenty years, I have taught the people who are preparing to be their teachers. In this capacity, I go out to the schools where they are, sit in the back of the classroom, and observe—much like a field biologist studying wildlife in the bush.

In the meantime, I raised three of them at my house. Maybe one of the reasons I like them now is that I don't have to take them home with me and live with them when the day is over.

Through these thirty–five years of observation and interaction with these animals we call "the early adolescents," I have begun to record certain patterns in their behavior and language; and some of it has even begun to make sense to me. That's why I dare tackle this topic of middle school reasoning. Understanding them is a bit like learning a foreign language. The sounds are familiar, but the nuances and hidden meanings require learned translation.

For the parents and others who read this book, I have two objectives. The first is a sense of *comraderie*. As people, who through some quirk of nature find yourself living with middle schoolers, you hold membership in a very special club, and you need to be reassured that you have company.

Each of the fifty topics covered here begins with a short description of some exchange. You can readily ascertain that I didn't make these up, nor did I gather them by looking through the keyhole at your house. These scenes are typical—could we even say normal? They occur in millions of homes across the country every day. Regardless of how bizarre your situation may seem, be comforted to know that you are not alone.

Some scenes will have immediate application to your family life. Some may not seem so relevant. But read on anyway. If you aren't seeing this particular behavior today, there is always tomorrow.

My second objective is *like*. I'm not going to admonish you to love them. You do that already, but that's the easy part. I would hope that somewhere in the relationship, you might develop a little like. Once you get to know them, they are rather interesting people and can be downright funny at times.

For your convenience, I have divided the fifty topics into four general categories: Friends, Family, Growth, and School. But these aren't distinctive entities. They all run together to create one life and one young individual trying to make sense of it in a special kind of way.

As you read through the book, you will begin to discover a pattern of themes. These are the themes of their lives and are worth noting here.

The first is *change*. Theirs is a world of change. Everything about them changes— their bodies, their friends, their relationship with the family, their demands, their expectations. Change leads to confusion, to trial and error, to misunderstanding.

Notice that we don't even have a name for them. Even that changes. We have children and we have teenagers, but these people are neither. So how do we identify them as we tell someone about the members of our household—Middle schoolers? Junior highers? Early adolescents? Sixth graders? Twelve-year-olds?

Some will question my choice of title for this book, but even in that we demonstrate the changing and confusing world these people have to navigate.

The next theme is *harshness*. They live in a much tougher world than we did when we were that age. It's a world of drugs, sex, crime, and scandal. But worse than that for them, it's a world of good people gone bad and a world where heroes are self-ish and immature. At a time when they demand concrete representations of abstract ideals, they have to search through lots of garbage to find the models.

The third theme is *temporariness*. Early adolescence isn't a permanent condition; it's even curable. In fact, in the scope of a lifetime, they don't stay here very long. Twenty years from now, this age will only seem like a distant speck to you. The only reminder you will have of what you went through will be some of your grandchildren who will be doing to their parents what those parents once did to you.

And all this leads us to the one conclusion that carries us all through parenthood and life. Surely God has a sense of humor.

PART 1

Friends

"But, Mom, Everybody will be there. Just Everybody!"

Isn't that sad? When they mix in a few tears and sobs, they can break your heart with this kind of talk, and you go to bed and have nightmares of all those innocent adolescents having fun at this party and your child is the only one in school not there. How can you be so cruel?

But don't despair. *Everybody* is a proper noun here. In other words, *Everybody* is only one person. Listen for a moment because this may be the best news you have heard for a while. Ever since it first dawned on you that this child was going to be leaving the neighborhood climate of the elementary school and moving to that fearful place called middle school, you have been worried sick that that nebulous monster called "Peer Pressure" was lurking in the halls ready to gobble up your innocent offspring.

You have every right to worry, but let me offer a bit of counsel. Peer pressure is not an amorphous horde of teenagers plotting against mankind. Peer pressure is one person—the person your child looks up to. And that person's name is Everybody.

Isn't this good news? You don't have to worry about something you can't identify or even influence. Sure, peer pressure exists; and, of course, it has power and influence over your child—what he does, what he thinks, and even what he feels. But peer pressure is within your realm of understanding, if not controlling.

Of course, there may be and probably is a group to which your child belongs so you get the idea that it is bigger than one individual; but if you study the situation closely, you will probably find one person who is the central leader and the spokesperson for the whole group. So it isn't the group that's peer pressure, but it's that one person—that one person we call Everybody.

My advice is obvious. Find out who Everybody is. Get acquainted with Everybody. Invite him over to the house. Take him on family outings. Make sure Everybody knows your family values and your expectations. If at all possible, get Everybody on your side. As I said before, Everybody has a great deal of influence on your child just now. Take this person seriously, but make the effort to get to know him.

Now let's go further. Make the effort to get to know Everybody's parents. Call them on the phone and ask them if it is true that Everybody is going to the party. It could well be that Everybody is at home even now pleading with his parents by telling them that your child is going and all the while referring to your child as Everybody. Invite Everybody's parents over and cultivate a close friendship with them. This in itself may well be the best time you can spend during this stage of your child's development. Your children will probably accuse you of forming a conspiracy, but a conspiracy is not all bad for parents of middle school children.

A few years ago, a group of parents of seventh grade girls took this suggestion even one step further and started meeting informally about once a month on Sunday evenings. At first they didn't know each other but came together with one common interest. They had daughters in the same class. Not only did they all grow into good friends, but these meetings went a long way to ease the anxiety of being the parent of an adolescent girl. In other words, they took an active instead of a reactive role to the threat of peer pressure.

"Oh, gross! Everybody really _is_ doing it!"

"Could you just make me a peanut butter and jelly sandwich?"

"But, Dear, why don't you eat in the cafeteria? You don't even like peanut butter and jelly."

"Oh, the nerds eat in the cafeteria."

This isn't about lunch. It could be about time. For a lot of students, the lunch period just isn't long enough. It sounds all right. They have thirty minutes, but when they stand in line for twenty of those minutes before they get their food, it just doesn't leave much time for them to eat and get back to class on time.

But this is probably more about socialization. School is a lonely place for many students. They go to class and sit among complete strangers—people they see every day but never learn their names and never have any kind of conversation with. This feeling of isolation in a crowd is bad enough in class, but because class isn't a social event anyway, the students make it through.

But lunch is a different story. In all your life you have never walked up to a complete stranger in a restaurant and said, "Move over, I want to sit here and eat my meal."

But this is what your child will have to manage if he is to eat in the cafeteria. What's even worse, many of the tables have already been formed with cliques of friends, and your child could well become a complete table isolate or even a reject before the meal is over.

School is often lonely, but lunch is the killer. This request is your child's way of saying that he either doesn't have many friends at school or his friends are on a different lunch schedule.

This may be a bit difficult to comprehend at first. He had friends in elementary school. He knew almost everybody, and they all moved to middle school together. Of course, people from six other schools came to middle school at the same time. But why can't he just stay in his old friendship group until he establishes himself in new ones?

It does sound simple, but for some reason, it doesn't work this way. That middle school experience has a way of scrambling everybody, and new friendship groups get formed almost immediately. The new groups tend to become highly structured, close-knit, and closed.

They organize around common activities such as church groups, club groups, or sports; and anyone not in that activity is an outsider with no place to sit at the table, no welcome seat on the bus, and not much role in class.

That's where your son is now.

The obvious solution to this problem is to help your child get acquainted with a wider variety of people. But that is easier to say than to carry out. Engineering friendships for your child is at best risky business and could be very dangerous. But if you think you need to give it a try, don't think in terms of school. There isn't all that much socialization in school anyway.

These new friendship groups almost always form around a common activity, so if you want your son to get into a group, you need to get him into an activity. Which activity he joins goes a long way to determine what kinds of friends he will have. In other words, football players have friends from the football teams. And band members have friends from band. People from the First Baptist Church youth group have friends from First Baptist Church.

So now you have a choice. You can either pack him a lunch or attempt to get him interested in some activity so that he can make enough friends to have company in the cafeteria.

Finally your son brings home his new friend from middle school; you don't like the guy. You feel like screaming, "With a thousand kids up there, why did you have to bring that one home for a friend?"

L et's begin by asking you a couple of questions. Do you pick your friends? Of course you don't. You get thrown together into situations and friendships grow out of the arrangement. Now for the second question. Do you have friends that you don't like very much? Well, so does your son, and this is probably one of the chief persons on the list. Try asking.

"Is that guy your friend?"

"Yeah."

"Do you really like him?"

"Not much."

"Well, why is he your friend?"

"I don't know. He's the only friend I've got. Just leave me alone."

And that's that. When he is this age, friends are necessary, and this is the only prospect he has.

For one thing, there may be a thousand kids at that school, but your son does not know them. There just aren't that many opportunities for him to meet people. He has no time to hang around his locker. Talk in class is forbidden so he never meets his classmates. Lunch is lonely. So where would he meet anybody?

Please take time out to ponder this. Parents of middle schoolers are deathly afraid of the peer pressure their children will encounter and the friends they will make.

And those are valid fears. But keep in mind there just aren't that many opportunities for your son to meet people.

Regardless of what your family values and expectations are, I would venture to guess that there are students at that school with the very same values and expectations. Those are the people you want your son to meet and develop friendships with. But how does he find them?

Every day, parents tell me, "My daughter's friends are all promiscuous. My son's friends smoke marijuana." I don't doubt those reports, and they scare me. But I still maintain that there are students at the school who aren't promiscuous and who don't take drugs. How do we find them and get them together?

Don't hold your breath until it happens. As we said in the previous chapter, you can put your son into some activities and hope that he meets people; but in the meantime, you have to deal with the situation at hand. He has a friend, and that friend has influence over your son.

Your first task, and a difficult one, is to try not to show your displeasure with his choice–not directly nor subtly. To do so could cause some really negative results.

Sometimes your child will bring a friend home just to check your reaction. If you show shock, you will only reinforce his choice.

But if this isn't his motive, your showing displeasure could cause him to doubt his judgment and to develop a defense to save face. "You don't trust me" is a common response. Then you have the really difficult task of trying to prove to him that you do trust him in such matters as choosing friends.

Your second task, and another difficult one, is to reinforce your son's sense of self-worth, dignity, and personal values so that he will not forsake his own personhood in the name of friendship. Of course this takes time and effort. But nobody ever promised you that being the parent of a middle schooler was easy.

"But, Mom, we have to go to the mall tonight."

**"But, Dear, it's snowed thirty inches.
We can't get to the mall."**

**"I don't care. I'm going to the mall even if I
have to crawl there on my hands and knees."**

You've already figured out that this is not about going to the mall. It's not even really about friends. This is about the concept of friendship, and that is one of the most powerful needs working in your child's life just now.

But this is even about more than friendship. It's about self-concept—feeling secure and competent and successful. All of us need to feel secure and competent and successful, and when we aren't feeling that way, we do whatever it takes to restore our confidence in ourselves and take charge of our lives again.

Most of us adults have this down to an exact science. We have been through bad days and bad periods so often that we know just what it takes to overcome self-doubt. We do our job really well; we make the big sale; we clean the house; we complete a task; we get out the hobby; or we achieve something.

These early adolescents haven't mastered the science yet, and most of them don't have all these methods and techniques at their disposal. So, for them, a successful life is succeeding in friendship. Thus, the goal of friendship is demanding and compulsive. If they agreed to meet friends at the mall tonight, meeting friends at the mall tonight is the most important event in the history of mankind. Not to meet friends at the mall tonight will cause feelings of failure, disloyalty and, worst of all, a feeling of rejection.

Don't try reason because, as you know from your own experience, reason does not do much good during times of despondency. It's not a reasonable time. It's a time of feelings and trying to keep feelings positive.

I wish I had some good suggestions for how to handle this mall situation because it could get ugly tonight. You might get a temper tantrum or whatever persuasive device the child decides to try, and you're on your own with those, but it is important that you understand the motive. Friendship is not a mere consequence or a pleasant possibility. Friendship is a necessary and all–compelling urge at this point. Going to the mall is just one symptom. Now you need to consider what other times and other conditions might cause your child to throw reason to the wind and take drastic measures to meet the demands of friendship.

"Just say no" is a nice little phrase, and it works well for many young people most of the time. But having that little phrase tucked away in a person's moral decision–making apparatus is probably not enough to overcome the compelling demands of friendship and self–concept at the precise moment when those demands come. You need to understand that before you ever let your teenager leave the house.

The solution to all this sounds simple enough, but it is probably the most difficult and risky part of being a parent. Help your child have a good self–concept so that he doesn't have to rely on friendship to fulfill his basic psychological needs. Sounds easy, doesn't it?

But this is a starting place. Your child needs to go to the mall tonight to achieve a feeling of approval and understanding. Does he know that you approve of him and understand him?

"Hey, Mom! I think I won't go to youth group anymore. I don't know those people."

There are three kinds of young people in our churches—those who don't attend youth group meetings, those who do attend, and those who enthusiastically participate. Because of the nature of church offerings and because of our desire to be supportive of the church, most of us as parents really want our children to be a part of that third group. But some aren't, and there are reasons for that.

In looking at those reasons, the first point we have to accept is that this may not have anything whatsoever to do with Bible study or Christian discipleship. It is quite possible for your child to mature and grow as a Christian outside the youth group.

Now that we've established this point of assurance, you still need to ponder why your child is wanting to move from group two to group one. It could be the very nature of the activities of youth groups themselves. Some teenagers just aren't all that interested in overnight rockathons, handing out tracts at the mall, or even attending meetings. Some teenagers have more interests than they have time, and since youth group activities aren't all that important to them, they make a choice not to participate fully. Then they soon lose interest in the group altogether.

But the biggest reason that church young people lose interest in the youth group is social. For all of its other reasons for existing and functioning such as Bible study, Christian activity, and worship, the first and foremost function of a youth group is to provide a circle of friendship and a sense of group belonging to these people at a stage in their lives when they desperately need friends and belonging. When the young person doesn't get this social interaction and sense of fitting in at church, he prefers to spend his time elsewhere.

The biggest factor to this socialization is the school attended. Every time I say this in public, church leaders descend on me en masse and protest that I don't know what I'm talking about and the situation doesn't really apply to their church. But it does, and I have never seen an exception. Church youth groups serve one school. Regardless of how many schools the students come from, the church still puts major emphasis on one school. The youth pastor visits one school more than the others. The majority of members of the youth group come from one school; thus, the leaders, both official and unofficial, come from that school. The people from the youth group hang out with each other at school. They develop inside jokes and inside stories. As a result of all this, they come together as a close–knit and functioning circle.

The person in the youth group who doesn't go to that school is on the outside. Regardless of what the church does to prevent this, it happens.

I would never advise a family to go church hopping, but you do need to know about this phenomenon. If you have children who are entering the middle school years, you need to know which school is most dominant in the church youth group; and if it isn't the school your child attends, you need to prepare yourself for the time when he comes to ask your permission to quit.

"If you have to take me to school, can you stop two blocks away and let me walk the rest of the distance?"

O h, this is simple. She's ashamed of her parents. You've seen it in other forms. She pleads for the family to go to the movies together. Then she bolts from the car, goes in alone, sits ten rows ahead of you, meets you back at the car, and talks of the fine family outing.

What other explanation can we give to this kind of behavior? If you want to call it being ashamed, I guess that's a good enough word, but I do think there are some deeper feelings going on here. She isn't really ashamed of you; she just doesn't know how to explain you.

For one thing, the cameras are on. Everybody is watching and taking notes and talking behind her back. She spent three hours this morning getting herself into the right look, and there just isn't enough time for her to get you spruced up enough to meet her friends' expectations. Thus, this is the simple solution.

Then there is this problem of being independent. Middle school is the time when she is strong enough to take the world on by herself. She doesn't need any help from anybody, and for her friends to see her with parents would require just too much explanation. It would make her look dependent and weak, and she can't have that.

Finally, there is this problem of the awkwardness of customs and manners. Suppose you meet her friends. How is she going to introduce you? She learned the format of introductions in English class, but she still doesn't remember which comes first—your name or her friend's name. What if you meet a teacher? Or even worse, what if you meet the principal and she isn't sure she remembers his name?

And what does she call you? "This is my mom." "Please meet my mother." "May I present Mrs. Jones?" It's all so awkward and the possibility of complete embarrassment is lurking behind every word. Frankly, I like her solution just to stay out of these situations as much as possible.

Now that I've said all this, I still don't know whether I've come close to explaining what's going on in the minds of middle schoolers when they act ashamed of their parents. But be assured. It's a natural and almost universal phenomenon. You're not the only parent worrying about it. The other day I chatted with a girl waiting outside the school for her mother to come to pick her up. The seemingly mature young lady expressed a real and great fear. "Oh, I hope she doesn't come in the generic car."

The other good piece of counsel is that this isn't terminal. She'll live through it. Why don't you write the statement down and document it with the date she said it. Then you can quote it to her as you are walking her down the aisle to give her away in marriage. That should bring some levity to the solemnity of the occasion.

In her most grown-up voice she pleads,
"Can I go? Can I? He's got his own car and all.
You won't even have to drive us."

O h, oh! It's the older friend syndrome, and it's time to panic. This disease can cut across several gender lines—guy to guy; girl to girl; guy to girl—but the younger girl to the older guy is the most frightening one of all.

The reasons for it are obvious enough. Perhaps she looks a little older. Perhaps she acts a little older than the other girls. But there is that strong possibility that she is, at least in some ways, more mature than her male colleagues. Usually eighth grade girls are interested in guys and eighth grade guys are interested in baseball and "Star Trek." Thus, if the girls are going to get any of their interests fulfilled, they will have to attract the attention of older boys, and parents cringe.

The big question here is just how big is the age difference. Of course, all this depends on the individuals, but age difference at this stage of growth is significant and varied. Let's put it in simple terms. A sixteen-year-old is a fifth of a lifetime older than a thirteen-year-old. Regardless of how and where the two of them have lived their lives, that's significant. The sixteen-year-old has been around more mature people; has been in more mature conversations; has watched television and listened to the music an additional three years; and has somewhat of a different outlook on life.

The next question we need to ponder is why is an older guy interested in a younger girl? What are his motives and what does he expect from the relationship?

Why does he find her company more appealing than the company of girls his own age?

The third question is how long will he be interested in her, and who is going to be around to pick up the pieces when the relationship crumbles? There is probably nothing more painful than being a jilted eighth grader except being the parents of a jilted eighth grader.

Now that we have decided that at best this situation demands caution, how do we proceed? To forbid her to go with the older guy would seem like the simple solution, but it has dangers. For some mysterious reason, making things taboo has a way of making them romantic; to forbid her going might make her urge to go with him even greater. The last thing you want to do is to create a situation where she goes out against your knowledge and will.

You might try reason. Sit down with her and have a long discussion. Ask all the right questions so that she feels she has had a satisfactory opportunity to examine her emotions and explain them to you. After that, you can give advice. On the surface, this sounds like a desirable approach, but as we all know, it has its limitations. Matters of the heart are never reasonable, but matters of the heart are especially unreasonable when you are thirteen years old.

The third approach would be to find a compromise. If she is determined to go and refuses to accept reason, then put some restrictions on your permission. The least you can do is to establish a definite time frame and demand that your time frame be honored. The next thing you need to do is to insist on meeting the older friend; you need to be honest with this person. Make sure he or she knows what your reservations and expectations are. The other possible restriction would be to insist on a group activity. In other words, she can travel in the company of this older person as long as someone else is with them. This requirement should put some limits on the relationship and bring some peace to parents.

She cries herself to sleep every night,
and the reason is always the same.
"Nobody likes me. I have no friends."

L oneliness is the disease of the age. The most popular girl in school cries herself to sleep because nobody likes her. The little inconspicuous girl who is known by no one does the same thing.

One of the reasons for this is that friendship really is fickle. It is probably fickle for all of us, but it is especially fickle for young adolescents. They are so fraught with self-doubt anyway that they tear apart each word, each piece of body language, and each nuance of every relationship. They start the day questioning whether they have friends and where they fit into the group; but as time progresses, they pick up some rather positive vibes, and they come home assured that they fit in. But as they play the day through in their minds at night, they begin to doubt again. And they cry themselves to sleep.

A middle school counselor tells me that this happens every day of the school year. At least one girl will come into his office each morning before school crying that she is a lonely outcast. He promises to speak to her friends about it, but he gets busy and forgets. As the crying one leaves in the afternoon, she stops by again and thanks him for fixing things up for her. The man says his forgetting has earned him the reputation of being one of the best middle school counselors in the nation. And this is the life of middle school friendships.

Another problem is the type of friendship patterns these people expect or perhaps even need. Most of us adults have several friends which we keep dangling on various strings of interest simultaneously. We also recognize that our friends have several friends too so that we don't have to entertain them every moment of the day.

But middle school people, at least some of them, tend to look at friendship a bit differently. They want one friend, one special friend, and they want all of that person's friendship. They don't want to share. They don't want their best friend to go to the mall with someone else or eat in the cafeteria with another group. This is tantamount to being jilted or rejected. They state their case by saying, "Nobody likes me." But that might be translated, "I just caught my best friend speaking to another person."

Another mystery is how they select a certain person to be their best friend, and they won't settle for anyone else. If 100 people adore your daughter, but the one she wants as a friend ignores her, she still cries, "Nobody likes me. I have no friends."

I have come face to face with this when I have tried to engineer friendships. I will have a little clique of girls in my class who have bonded tightly and shut out everyone else. Yet, I have one little lonely girl isolated in one corner and another little lonely girl isolated in the other corner. In my best logical mind I decide that those two girls can become friends with each other. Now doesn't that make sense? So I engineer the group work project so that those two have to work closely together for several days.

When that idea fails dismally, I realize that they don't want to be friends with each other. They want to be friends with those girls in the clique.

I tried my best, but I'm sure they cried themselves to sleep at night while their parents stood outside the door and worried.

***Bad news. The assistant principal just called.
Your son, the quiet one who never has all that much
to say, started a food fight in the cafeteria.***

They are a laugh a minute! Or at least a surprise a minute!

After you recover from your shock, conquer your urge to kill him, can think about it without feeling terribly guilty, and go to the school to be a part of the retribution process, you can pause to ponder what went wrong. You can ponder, but you may never come to much of a satisfactory conclusion.

Maybe he did it in the name of socialization. In other words, he did it to impress someone. This does happen. People like your son want to be a part of a group, so they throw caution and training to the wind and do something stupid in the name of friendship. These people are often urged on, while the ringleader sits back and enjoys the chaos he caused without suffering any of the consequences.

At this point, you really need to know in which relationships your son is a leader and in which he is a follower. Which ringleaders will he follow and which can he avoid? For this information consult one of his teachers.

Maybe your son didn't mean to start a food fight. He was calmly eating his lunch when someone bumped his elbow causing him to spill milk on the person next to him. That person retaliated with a handful of mashed potatoes, and the riot began.

This is not a far–fetched theory. Middle schools can be very tense places. There is a large number of people in a rather small place. They have to sit still for hours. They are often thrown into embarrassing or vulnerable situations.

The surprise is not that innocent little acts erupt into rather serious events. The surprise is that it doesn't happen more often then it does.

And it can all be caused by a completely innocent person.

For example, one student was trying to impress a girl and leaned against the wall to appear cool. Unfortunately, he leaned against the fire alarm, and set the thing blaring, causing the building to be evacuated and the fire trucks to come roaring out. This cost his parents $200, and all he was trying to do was impress a girl.

Maybe your son started the food fight and has no idea why he did it. At this age, boys and girls do things they can't explain. There are times when the body parts work independently of the brain. They are just sitting around when the mouth says something all its own. They hadn't thought about it; they weren't planning to say it. It just came out. We adults can understand this. We, too, sometimes have words come out of our mouth which surprise and embarrass us.

But they have these involuntary outbursts of hand and feet as well. For some unknown reason, the foot kicks somebody. It wasn't premeditated. It just happened. The foot acted on its own.

As wise counselors and philosophers of ethics, we get dizzy trying to analyze this.

"Why did you dump your plate on that boy?"

"I dunno."

"Do you know him?"

"A little bit."

"Do you like him?"

"I guess."

"Had he done something to you?"

"No."

"So why did you dump your plate on him?"

"Because."

And that is middle school reasoning.

"I can't wear this.
You bought it at Kmart."

Don't be harsh until you've thought through this. It has nothing to do with her being an ungrateful, elitist snob. It is simply a statement about the middle school costume code.

You really need to know about the code. Reading it and digesting it can save you heartache and frustration, not to mention the money you waste by buying her things she won't wear. The problem is that the code isn't published anywhere. They just make it up, and often they make it up month by month and week by week. How are you supposed to know what's on the code? Read her mind.

The code seems to be based on a philosophy of collective individualism. Somehow together middle schoolers establish the rules of the code right down to the most minute detail—where you bought it, how much you paid for it, how to tie it, and how low to sling it. Then they attire themselves within this precise and narrow set of rules and restrictions. But they do all this as a way to express their own unique individuality, and to deny them compliance of costuming would be to infringe on their individual rights as a person and as an American.

Where the code originates is something of a mystery. Sometimes one popular leader can rewrite the code according to her whims and tastes, but more often it seems to come out of some informal group agreement where the group has some input from a popular television program or a current movie. Consequently, there are several codes at work in one building at once. The one you need to know about is the one that incorporates your daughter.

In the past few years, we've all heard horror stories about the requirements of the costuming code and the lengths some children go to comply. There are tales of $150 shoes, $250 jackets, and a refusal to wear anything from a discount store of any kind. All this comes at a time when their bodies are changing so rapidly that it is difficult for almost all parents to keep up with just the financial demands of clothing those ever-growing bodies.

School officials have recognized the problem this presents, and throughout the country, there is talk of the possibility of adopting school uniforms for middle schools. This is one possible solution to the problem.

But we do need to move cautiously. As she lectures you on where to buy it and what label it should have on the pocket, listen carefully to her tone and reasons. There is more here than just simply spending a lot of money. At a time when the body isn't all that dependable, when friendships change as often as the weather pattern, and she really can't find much about herself that she likes, following that costume code is one small form of consistency and dependability—one way to be an individual fitting into a group.

This is the real code, and the appropriate costume is a symbol of that.

PART 2

Family

You always wanted her to be a ballerina; you dreamed of it; and you have had her in lessons since she was four. But now she wants to quit ballet and try out for the basketball team. Probably the thing that bothers you the most is that she isn't destined for stardom in ballet anyway.

This could be the ugliest part of being a parent. It may well be the scariest part of being a parent of a middle schooler. This is a time when all of us have to accept reality, and sometimes reality is hard to deal with.

As soon as they are born, we begin to dream for them. That is both the duty and the privilege of being a parent. When they are babies, we can dream big dreams—the bigger the dreams the better. What's the harm in this? They're just dreams.

When they get a little bigger, we begin to put some action to our dreams. We put them in special classes and give them training, motivation, and our dreams.

But about the time they enter middle school, we have to come face to face with the reality that when God made this person, He specifically chose the gifts and abilities that He wanted her to have. What hurts is that God has not always chosen the gifts that we parents wanted her to have and that we've dreamed about all these years. That's the rub.

When our children move through those early teens, a variety of factors have the potential to strain the parent–child relationship, but it's probably not fair for us to attribute all those factors to the children. Unless we are completely honest with ourselves, this issue here can become one of the major sources of contention. We just have to accept the truth that maybe our child doesn't have the God–given gifts to become what we want her to be.

My son was in the eighth grade when I first realized that he would never win the Heisman trophy for being the best football player in the nation. To be honest, I have to admit that I felt a bit cheated, and I probably found some way to show that to him. Now that my son is a professional man and, more important, a good father, I'm so happy with him. I'm especially happy that I didn't make his football playing the core of our relationship during those years when I had to deal with reality.

So your daughter is never going to become a great ballerina. That's all in God's plan. Now accept her, encourage her, and even give her the support for what she chooses with the same enthusiasm you supported her when she was fulfilling your dreams. And praise God for the gifts He chose to give her.

"Hey, Mom. Dad said it was all right with him for me to sleep over at Michelle's, so I've already packed."

O h, oh. You're in trouble now, aren't you? She's discovered the old divide-and-conquer trick, and it seems as if she's going to use it effectively. Notice that she started with Dad. Most girls tell me that you always start your request with Dad. He's much softer than Mom is. At least, that's what the scouting report says.

Actually, I'm not sure I blame kids for using this technique. Sometimes we parents deserve it. How many times have we forced them into this?

"Dad, can I go to Michelle's?"

"I don't know, Dear. Ask your mother."

"Mother, can I go to Michelle's?"

"I don't know, Dear. It all depends on what your dad says."

Before long the young people figure out this runaround, and they find some way to short-circuit it.

But with middle schoolers, we need to look even deeper at this method. If you have children at this age, it is absolutely important that Mom and Dad say exactly the same thing and read from the same manual on expectations and discipline.

In order to give this proper emphasis, let me state it again. Regardless of your family situation, it is imperative, necessary, and an absolute requirement that Mom and Dad speak with one voice.

In the midst of their chaos, middle schoolers are searching for and pleading for something consistent. The least we can do for them is to provide them with a consistent set of family rules, expectations, and consequences. This is a parental obligation which can not be forgiven.

If you and your spouse have not come together on middle school issues yet, it is time to do it and the hour is urgent. Take a weekend if you have to, but come to an agreement. Anticipate as many situations as you can. Just for starters, deal with the following:

1. When will they date and how?
2. What grades do you expect?
3. What expectations do you have for friends?
4. When is curfew and what happens when it is violated?
5. What is the dress code?
6. What are the requirements for church attendance?

After you and your spouse have discussed that anticipated list, you must decide which one of you will respond to those sure-to-come situations which even in your wildest dreams you couldn't imagine. But whatever it takes, agree to be one voice.

Last weekend I attended a high school graduation and watched Amy walk across the stage. This was a particularly moving experience.

When Amy was in eighth grade, she developed a strong dislike for her English teacher, and her solution for dealing with her emotions was not to do her work. She reasoned that this would spite her teacher.

Amy was right. The teacher was offended and asked to meet with her and her parents.

Both parents came, pledged their support, and helped develop a strategy for helping Amy over this tough spot.

Several weeks later the teacher discovered that Amy's parents were divorced, but they had put aside their differences long enough to come to a parent–teacher conference with a common objective.

And Amy is an honor graduate.

"Dad, make her be quiet so I can study in here."

"But, Dear, why don't you go to your room and study?"

*"I don't want to. I want to study in here.
Will you make her be quiet so I can concentrate?"*

This is indeed a rich family and this is such a positive plea. We all ought to rejoice.

Most of us parents grew up watching way too much "Leave It to Beaver," and we're all carried away with this idea of family and space. We have unconsciously come to the conclusion that one of the emblems of middle class success is to have a house big enough for each child to have a room of her own so that each child can retire into the haven of that room and take care of all personal business. After all, that's the way the Cleaver family did it.

But this is real life, and real life doesn't imitate the Cleavers. In good families, there is some designated space in the house that I call the "family altar." This is where family takes place. It's where the family meets, shares together, plays together, and makes decisions together. But more important than all that, this is where you go when you want to feel that you belong to the family and that you have support and help in handling the outside world.

I have no idea how specific spots in the house get designated as the family altar. Sometimes it's the kitchen table; sometimes it's the TV room. When our children were at home, family took place in our bedroom. If I had known about this concept and had time to think about it, I might have tried to engineer some other place. We had regular meetings on our bed. We would meet at the bed when we got up in the morning and again before we went to bed at night. We would often wake up in the middle of the night to find some child huddled in a corner doing homework by flashlight.

We may find this at first some kind of a nuisance, but it's a nuisance worth living with, and twenty years from now, you'll praise God for it. If this child has a need to study in this room, help as much as you can.

In order for there to be a nuclear family, there has to be a nucleus—a hub, a center, a core around which everybody in the family moves and takes their place. This family altar is probably not the nucleus, but it is at least a symbol of it. Something positive is going on here, and this child feels it and needs to be a part of it just now. At this time in her life when her whole world is in change and turmoil, she needs to be in one spot where everything is familiar and comfortable.

That's why she had to study here tonight. It's all right for you to shush the sibling because tomorrow the roles will be reversed, and you'll be shushing tonight's complainer.

Your seventh grader has just quit communicating with you. She's pleasant enough, but you would like to have some report about what's going on in her life.

As the wise philosopher once said, "What goes around comes around," and communicating with our children is just one of the experiences in the circle of life. Sometimes they talk so much that we think they will never shut up, and they recite details that we really don't care that much about hearing. But then they go through this period when any little peep would be welcome news. This may be one of the most frustrating factors in being a parent of an adolescent. When they were children, we thought we understood them because they talked enough to give us a bit of insight into their brain and soul, but while they are in adolescence, it's all guesswork—not one single clue as to what they might be thinking.

I'm not sure I totally understand this, but it may have something to do with their changing attitude toward us. At one time, they thought we were infallible and omniscient. "My daddy can whip your daddy." "My mommy is the smartest lady in the world and the most beautiful." Can you recall those glorious days of old? Wasn't it wonderful? We knew their perceptions weren't true, and we probably knew deep down inside that one day they would discover the truth, but there isn't any need to argue with childlike appraisal.

But in adolescence, they change their mind. In fact, they take the opposite side. When they discover that we really aren't the smartest people in the world, they then surmise that we must be the dumbest people in the world, and we have to go through a few years of that false perception.

Don't panic. This too is natural and temporal. If you don't follow through on some of your sudden impulses to annihilate them and you do let them grow up, they will someday come to a rather accurate appraisal of your talents and intelligence, and they will accept you and love you for what you really are.

In the meantime, we have to live with this attitude that we aren't worthy of their conversation. Maybe their minds are working so fast on a variety of topics that they don't have time to talk to us. Maybe they have picked up some real or imaginary hint that we don't care. Maybe they are just so engrossed in themselves that it is hard for them to reach inside themselves and figure out enough of what they are thinking to share it with us.

But I have a tip. I offer this to you with almost a money–back guarantee. It never fails to work. If you really want to know what this girl is thinking, learn to eaves-drop. And you can do it legally too. Load her and a friend of hers in the backseat of the car; then you get in the front seat and drive them around town. I don't know why this is, but two seventh graders in the backseat of a car assume that the adult in the front seat is deaf, so they chatter constantly. Almost everything I know about middle schoolers I learned while hauling them around in the car while I drove and listened.

After laundering his jeans,
you find a condom in the washer.

If you keep your calm in this situation, you should travel the country giving seminars on self-control. Let's be honest. This is panic time—the time we all dread; and I doubt that any of us are very reasonable. But let's think it through in the attempt to get a handle on what's happening.

There are three possibilities: (1) He needs a condom because he is using them. (2) He is thinking about using one. (3) He was just carrying it to impress his friends.

Regardless of the reason, we have to begin with a scary but obvious point. Your son is a sexual person. He may or may not be engaging in sex, but he is still a sexual person. He has the ability, and he has the urge. Regardless of how thoroughly we train our children or how much we pray for them, they aren't immune to growth or sexual urges. Oh, how we can wish it would never happen, but it does. It happens to them all, and we can't bury our heads in the sand and ignore it.

The next point is just as obvious. Your son knows far more about the subject than you think he does. He may be ignorant about it, but he isn't uniformed. Be assured that he isn't uninformed. If you want to test my point, check out a movie from thirty years ago. You will discover that there is more frank sexual reference on the ten o'clock news than there used to be in dirty movies. Your innocent little child has been exposed to this almost all of his life.

Let's try another test case. How old were you when you realized people used their tongues to kiss each other? Your son knew how to do that in the third grade.

Not only does he learn about sex from the media, he has friends; and they talk about sex. Some of his associates (I won't call them friends because they may not be in his close circle) are sexually active. Again, they may be ignorant about the subject, but they are still active. The topic comes up in your son's conversations.

Given these two points, you now have a choice. You can have your son get his information and values from the media and associates, or you can talk to him yourself. These are the only two possibilities I can think of. Some schools do have sex education classes, and some of these provide rather reliable information. But your son is going to get this information confirmed from some other source. And that's where you have to enter the picture.

It's easy for me to say this in such matter-of-fact language because he is your son and not mine. Parents tell me all the time about how they talk about sex with their children. Well, they're braver than I am because, frankly, I find this about the most difficult aspect of parenthood. You have to do it, but it is so hard.

First, you have to pick the right time. If you are as angry as I would be after having found the condom, don't choose this moment for a meaningful sex education talk. Choose a time when you can talk calmly.

Next, you have to talk on something of a mutual basis. Unlike a lot of conversations you have with your son where you are the boss and he is the peon, this conversation must begin with trust and sharing. You can talk, but he needs to feel free to talk too. Without his input, you will still live with fear and distrust.

The other characteristic of this discussion is that it has to be open-ended. The first objective of any conversation you have with your child about sex is to open the door to future conversations. Keep this in mind. Regardless of how you feel about your child right now, you must project the attitude that you are always open to hear his side of the issue. You may dread it, but it is still better for him to come to you instead of going somewhere else!

You would take an oath and swear that your thirteen-year-old daughter is the laziest person in the world. She refuses to clean her room by claiming American citizenship; she thinks that to carry her plate from the table to the sink would destroy her whole day; and yard work is for barbarians.

The neighbors hire her to babysit, and you dread the report, but when you hear it, you can't believe it: "Best little worker we ever had. She kept the children, cleaned the house, ironed the clothes, painted the garage."

Surprise! You've raised a nice person instead of a sniveling, complaining, sloppy sloth. Isn't that good news?

What do you do with this report? You take it and put it in your family bank. Don't doubt it, not for a moment. Don't argue. This is the accurate picture of your daughter, and the one you want to cherish.

The point here is obvious, but it's painful to accept. But since she's your daughter instead of mine, I'll make it anyway. Other people's opinions of your child are probably more accurate than yours. Oh, I hate to have to say that, but it's true. We all have to live with it.

Actually, this is probably how the family is supposed to work. Robert Frost wrote in "The Death of a Hired Man:" "Home is the place where, when you have to go there, they have to take you in." How about adding, "Home is where you can go and be grumpy if you need to." Be honest, wouldn't you rather have her lazy at home and a good worker away from home than the other way?

No one can be upbeat, cheerful, and industrious all the time. We all have our down moments and a strong resistance to the tasks at hand. It just seems to me that home is the best place to get that out of your system, and if your daughter feels that comfortable with you, I think you should be pleased with what you have accomplished in the name of family.

Of course, we would like our young adolescents to put family first in their lives, but they don't. This has something to do with their definition of responsibility. If they are getting paid for it in immediate and hard cash, the task is a real responsibility. If the rewards are long–term or abstract, they have trouble seeing the value of all that effort.

This leads us to another point. Because this is the way family works, it is essential that you have some reliable folks outside the family giving you accurate pictures of what your daughter really is like. Cultivate those reports from the neighbors about her work habits and skills. Develop a relationship with teachers who will tell you about her attitude at school, both around fellow students and other teachers.

Again, it's painful to admit, but as parents, we never know how our children relate to their peers or other adults. Every time we see them with another person, we are present and that changes the social dynamic. To take as much anxiety as we can out of being a parent, we need to have some idea of how they relate when we aren't around. That's the true picture.

Then we don't have to act too surprised when we discover that they aren't as lazy as we think they are.

He used to come sit on your lap and beg to be hugged; but since he turned thirteen, he hasn't let you close enough to touch him, much less, hug him.

Chase him down and hug him anyway. This standoffish role is partly real and partly a game. Just assume you can play the game too and hug him. On the outside, he will act a little put out with you, but that's part of the game too. He must communicate the image of being macho and tough even when he doesn't always feel macho and tough.

The value of your forcing a hug on him once in a while is to demonstrate to him that although he's changing and his world is changing, your relationship isn't changing. It is still built on love and honesty, and that hug is just one symbol of that. It assures him that you are there, and that you will do what it takes to be in his corner.

Right now, he lives his life among friends who don't have that assurance. Some of the stories he could tell you would shock you—stories of people who live with one parent three days a week and another parent four days a week, stories of classmates who have to move to a secluded part of the house because their parents don't want them around.

As he compares what he has at home to what his friends have at their homes, he has some confused emotions. Perhaps he feels a bit guilty. Or maybe, in a strange way, all this exotic living among his friends sounds a bit exciting and romantic. Regardless of how he interprets them, those stories are a real part of his being, and he wonders about life and stability.

So he decides to discover some emotional independence by resisting your hugs. He needs to know if he can make it on his own.

But this little experiment of his is only temporary. Throughout my career, I've enjoyed watching young people move in and out of different emotional relationships with their parents. They decide they are all grown-up and independent; then a couple of years later, they come back to us. For example, college freshman often deal with homesickness by becoming quite independent. They don't even go home on holidays and breaks. But four years later, they move back in with parents to spend the first two years of their career.

So, never close the lap. There will be times when our children don't seem to need the lap, but they will always come back. Being a parent is a lifetime mortgage. He may not act as if he needs your hug today, but twenty years from now, he will remember it, and he will chase down his son to hug him just as his parents taught him to do.

Wow, you got the big promotion! You're moving to the home office. This is the chance of your lifetime. More money, more prestige, more family fun. But what will the move mean to the eighth grader and the fourth grader?

Thanks for asking. As we have discussed throughout this book, children this age live in a world of constant change as it is. There isn't much about their world today which looks like their world of yesterday. In the midst of this change, they look for stability and consistency wherever they can find it. Many rely on their home life to provide this.

But one of the realities we have to accept is that we are a part of their changing world too. Our lives change; we go through cycles, periods and eras; and often some of our biggest change comes at that time when our children are in the throes of some of the greatest changes in their world.

Often people say, "I don't know how two children can come from the same home and be so different." But I'm not sure two children ever came from the same home. My wife asks me not to say this in public, but I have to admit it. We have three children, and they all had different fathers. I was a different person; my career was different; my interests were different; our family friends were different. If you asked my children to describe their father, you would probably get three different responses. All this reminds me that we parents are a part of others' change.

But you can't put your life on hold just because you have an eighth grader at home. You have to seize the opportunity, but you do need to be reminded that this is another source of trauma in your children's lives. They will make it, but your under–

standing will help them make it more easily.

Just changing houses can be a major ordeal. Although they may not act like it, they do get comfortable at home. There is something stabilizing in knowing where their toothbrush is and knowing exactly how many steps separate the upstairs from the downstairs.

Changing churches can also bring about some emotions. I once was teaching junior high Sunday School on the day the pastor announced his resignation. All the students cried, and I doubted their sincerity until I realized that he was the only pastor they had ever had. For them, their pastor was church, and church was one of the few dependable areas of their lives.

Changing schools can be a source of great frustration. But it isn't the school itself. It's the socialization. It is just plain hard for a newcomer to work herself into the friendship circles that have already been formed.

Now that you know this, you can make a mental list of things you can do to help make the transition easier for your children.

First, find something in your family life that is stable and consistent. Since all the visible factors are going through some change, you may have to manufacture something abstract. But find something—a common family vacation, a specific Saturday morning ritual, mealtime, family devotions. (If you have been meaning to do family devotions but have never quite gotten around to it, now is the perfect time to start.) This could be the one thing carried over from the old life to the new one that might just be the key to the children finding something consistent.

The other thing you need to pay particular attention to is providing some kind of opportunity for your children to meet fellow students before they start into their new schools. Let me state Schimmels' School Principle One: It is criminal to send a child to a school when the child doesn't know anyone at that school.

Do what you need to do—visit churches, invite neighbors over, go to ball games—so that your children will know someone when they enter that new world.

You agree that he will be
home at 11 P.M. on a Friday night.
He makes it at 12:02 A.M.

Punish him and punish him severely. He has it coming. There are actually two lessons for us parents in this little scene.

First, these people need boundaries. As parents, we have a right to set boundaries. Our children expect boundaries. I believe they want boundaries.

Let me explain that by telling a story. As a principal, I walked by a classroom in chaos. The young teacher was having a real struggle. Instead of going in and being obtrusive, I went down to the office and waited for a culprit. Chuck came, and I said, "Chuck, are you in trouble again?"

He answered matter-of-factly, "Yes, but it's not my fault. She can't control that classroom."

Impressed with his ability to shift blame, I explained, "But Chuck, I just came from there. You are the worst person in that class."

"I know," he reasoned. "She can't make me behave, and I shouldn't be in trouble for that."

The lesson is obvious. Children want us to make them behave. So we set the boundaries at an 11 P.M. curfew. And what do they do? They test the boundaries to see if they are real or just words. Now what do we do? We reaffirm the boundaries by punishing them so severely that they know this boundary is real and is never to be tested again. So what do they do? They cry and argue, "You don't trust me."

And to this we respond, "Yes, I do. I trust you, but I don't trust those other idiots out this time of night. And since I am the one old enough to have a heart attack if I don't get my way, you will be home at 11 o'clock from now on." Case closed.

The second lesson for parents in this is knowing which boundaries to set. In other words, draw your battle lines carefully. I have used the curfew because it is an issue dear to my heart. This is more my problem than theirs. I have a vivid imagination. If my chicks are not safely in the coop and nestled under my wing, I imagine all sorts of harm and despair for them. I can survive those imaginings until 11 P.M., but I'm not going to survive it any longer. They will be home when we agreed that they would!

But I don't feel that strongly about haircuts or homework or a couple of other issues. I know they expect boundaries, and I believe they want boundaries, but we are going to choose those boundaries together. When they get out of bounds, they can expect punishment, and then we will start all over again.

**"Hey, Mom.
I don't think I'll go to Grandma's house this Sunday.
I'll just stay home and watch TV."**

You've heard of double questions? Well, this is a triple statement. It has many levels of meaning.

Level one is a question, but it comes disguised as a declarative sentence. What she is really saying is, "Do I have to go to Grandma's house this Sunday?" Or maybe, "Could I even entertain the idea of not going to Grandma's house?"

I'm not sure I know why they ask questions in the form of declarative sentences, but it is a common speech pattern. I think it has something to do with limited language ability. It is just harder to form interrogatives, so they give you everything in a declarative.

It sounds abrasive, abrupt, and definite, but you have to learn to read into it "question" and maybe even "timid question." Respond accordingly.

Her question at level two is about boundaries or about the rules. This is probably not even a statement about whether she enjoys going to Grandma's house, so reasoning with her and trying to persuade her that there will indeed be something for her to do and that she will indeed have a good time is not going to be too effective. What she wants to know is what the rules require. Are you committed to this decision that she is going to go to Grandma's house? At this point, you need to decide whether or not you want to draw a battle line over this issue.

If you do insist, expect an argument. You may get a full-fledged argument with powerful logic, followed by tears and shrieks, followed by a temper tantrum. As you can tell, this is a test case, and she needs to know how strong the rules are.

If you decide that this isn't a big issue, and you tell her that it's all right for her to stay home, don't be too surprised if she decides to go anyway.

At level three, this is a question about her maturity and your opinion of it. She wants to know if you think she is mature enough to stay home from a family trip. She wants you to express your confidence in her. She thinks she's old enough, but she doesn't know whether you do, so she picks this spot to get an affirmation.

Discovering these boundaries is an absolute must for her. She needs to know just what kinds of decisions she is allowed to make on her own and what kinds of decisions still require your input and counsel. This is all a part of growing up, both for the child and for the parent.

When are we ready to trust them enough to turn loose? How do they know that we are ready to turn loose?

"Hey, Mom. Make her get out of my room and stay out of my room. I don't ever want her in my room again for the rest of my life."

Oh, the sweet sounds of sibling love! Don't you feel sorry for families with only one child? Those parents don't get to practice their skills of diplomacy and negotiation so they can identify with Jimmy Carter at his summit conferences. And the children don't get to practice their language skills as they try to manufacture the vilest names they can think of to label properly their loved ones.

Having one child in middle school and one or more of a different age provides a great opportunity for the educational development of everyone involved. It must have something to do with age difference. A twelve-year-old is at least fifteen years older than a ten-year-old; and a twelve-year-old is at least twenty years younger than a fourteen-year-old. All this makes the twelve-year-old suitable company for other twelve-year-olds but not even close to being on the same wavelength with anyone else.

Whatever the cause of those fights—independence, the pressure of the rest of life, intense change in size and mood, they still have a way of grating on family harmony. I know families where this whole thing is so severe that the family activity for the evening hinges on the prevailing mood of the middle schooler present.

There isn't any advice here because I've never met anyone who has learned how to handle these sibling fights and selfishness.

You can apply some therapy and order some boundaries which might work for a while, but you will have to do it all over again a couple of hours later.

But there is good news. Sibling relationships, like everything else, come in cycles. In a few years, she will grow out of her rivalry and territorializing stage and will assume the responsibility of helping you rear the younger sister. Actually, she won't get directly involved in the rearing, but she will appoint herself consultant. Then you will get the following: "Mother, do you know who her friends are? I really think you should be more concerned about her friends." "I can't believe you are letting her go, not at her age. When I was her age, you wouldn't let me go. You are going to get in trouble for being softer on her than you were on me."

The next cycle comes when they both grow up, leave home, move to different parts of the world, and become the closest friends. Then they run up huge telephone bills trying to catch up on all that conversation they missed out on when they were young and couldn't go into each other's rooms.

The crowning victory of familiness occurs at Christmas when they all come home. They are so glad to see each other that they spend all their time together and forget entirely about you and your life. Then you want to beat them on the head and remind them of those days you spent negotiating their expressed hatred of each other.

Isn't life fun?

"...And that was the year our daughter
started middle school."

"I guess if I have to have parents, I would just as soon have you guys as anybody else."

Wow! I'm impressed. This may be the greatest compliment you will ever get in your life. But you have to learn to accept it as that.

Diplomacy and tact are not affairs of the heart or even courtesy. Those things have to do with language skills. It doesn't matter how she feels. If she doesn't have sophisticated language to express those feelings, she comes across as curt and rude.

Diplomatic people say, "My, it seems that you carry your weight well." Middle schoolers say, "Hey, you're fat."

Diplomatic people say, "What an interesting combination of colors you have chosen." Middle schoolers say, "Your tie clashes."

Diplomatic people say, "I found your speech refreshing and interesting." Middle schoolers say, "I thought I would be bored, but I wasn't."

Diplomatic people say, "This was a good class." Middle school people hear the bell and say, "Already?"

My friend taught eighth grade the year his wife delivered their son. In a great show of tenderness, his students secretly collected money and bought a beautiful baby blanket. When they presented it to him during a class, he was almost in tears until one of the students established the ground rules. "If that baby dies, we get the blanket back." That's all part of the language problem.

It's hard to use words like *love, like, enjoy, appreciate,* and *admire.* In their time of concrete reality, these words carry deep meaning and shouldn't be flung about carelessly. Beyond the language difficulty, giving out compliments is difficult because it violates a couple of codes.

First, there is the code which says that people this age should never let anyone see that they care. They just can't show their true feelings.

I think it must have something to do with announcing to the world that they are vulnerable. So they hide those feelings the best they can.

You can recognize this by watching young adolescents at a movie, particularly if there is a group. If the movie is well done and riveting, and if they really do care about the characters, when the tragic moment comes and you would expect the appropriate emotion of sadness, they will probably laugh. The first few thousand times I heard that laughter, I thought it was cruel; but if you listen closely, you can detect that it is a nervous laughter. It is a false front to cover some true feeling.

By the same reasoning, a compliment, a genuine compliment which expresses true feelings, would show their vulnerability and their tenderness, so don't wait around eating your heart out until you get one. Go with what you have and cherish it as sincere.

The other code involved with the compliment is that middle schoolers are never supposed to admit that they like their parents. Just as college students have their code which prohibits their admitting that they like cafeteria food, these middle schoolers have their code too. To make a positive statement about parents would cause them to lose face and credibility. Not only would they not get to participate in the jokes and stories about parents, but they would become the butt of the jokes. And this is a terrible price to pay.

In her way, your daughter told you that she loves you. Just don't expect her to do it again.

PART 3

Growth

***He stands on tiptoe, looks you in the face, and declares,
"I'm as tall as you are."***

L et's be honest. Growth is important to them because growth is important to us. Let's suppose for a moment that you hire two seventh graders to come over to your house on a Saturday afternoon to help you with some yard work. When they show up, you find a typical duo. One is almost six feet tall and the other is almost five feet tall. To which one will you give the instructions?

See what I mean? We're prejudiced, and they sense it. We can talk all we want to about understanding Luke 2:52, which explains our Lord's growth in four ways—physical, mental, social, and spiritual, but the truth is that we expect physical growth to be a concrete symbol of all that other growth. In our expectations, taller seventh graders are more mature than shorter ones.

And this leads us to the mystery of the big problem. If we look at their parents, grandparents, and aunts and uncles, we can get a fairly accurate idea of how big children are going to be when they are all grown up, and we may even persuade them to accept our wisdom and prediction.

But this still doesn't explain the mystery of when they are going to grow. And that's the part that bothers them.

As we know, a lot of this growth is going to come in one giant spurt. But when is this spurt going to come? Every day they are around people who are spurting right before their eyes, and they see the results of this growth spurt. One day the guy is just another kid in P.E. class. Two weeks later he is the star of the basketball team. One day this girl has baby fat cheeks and pigtails. Two weeks later she looks eighteen, and all the older guys are asking her out. One day the teacher doesn't even remember this person's name. Two weeks later the teacher leaves him in charge when she leaves the room.

And the non–growing bystander says, "When is this growth and opportunity going to come to me?" I have known people who have almost panicked over this. They have waited so long to grow that they conclude God has overlooked them and they are never going to get any bigger.

So the little signs to measure size such as standing on tiptoe and comparing, or reaching around the wrist, or wanting to put marks on the door frame are not just casual requests. These are serious pleas for assurance and acceptance.

If your child is going through this stage, you may want to spend some time thinking through this whole business of four–way maturity, and you may want to rethink your assessment of his maturity and your expectations growing out of that assessment.

Your seventh grade son wants a paper route and is rather demanding about it. But you don't know whether he can get up at five o'clock every morning, and you really don't need the money.

I know what you're worried about. Paper routes are never singular. They are always plural. Within a matter of days, his paper route becomes our paper route with the shared responsibilities of getting up on time, folding the papers, and getting them delivered during the month he decides to have mono. I don't blame you for being concerned.

But let's look at the bigger picture. His desire or need here is a real one, and it isn't about money either. Human beings need to feel needed. We all need to feel that we are making some kind of a contribution to mankind—that we are not just eating the resources and breathing valuable air.

In earlier generations, children became economic assets to the family quite early in life. They milked cows, cut wood, carried out ashes, and performed semi-adult functions. Nowadays, we don't really need our children. In fact, rather than being economic assets, they are economic liabilities, and we tell them that. "Do you know how much a gallon of milk costs? Do you know how much our insurance will go up when you start driving?"

Here is your son, almost old enough to become a full–fledged money–making adult, and he needs to find out what that world is like. He wants to experience the emotions of having responsibility.

You would think that his family chores would satisfy that need. After all, you expect him to cut the grass, carry out the garbage, and even wash the dishes. But for some reason it doesn't work that way. These family responsibilities fall short of whatever it is that he is searching for. So he wants a paper route.

Having a paper route, like any job he could get, has some peril. He will have to get up early and go to school tired. He won't have as much time for his home-work. He won't get to eat a leisurely breakfast. Is it all worth it?

Well, you and he will have to answer that. There are plenty of horror stories of students who let work and responsibility stand in the way of school work and school activities. On the other hand, I know of hundreds of cases, like your son, where a part-time job was exactly what young adolescents needed in order to discover the next level of human growth and responsible action. Don't make generalizations here. Decide the case on its own merit.

Regardless of what you decide, at least understand your son's need for a paper route and come up with some way to fulfill that need.

"If I lived in Somalia, I wouldn't starve to death."
"What would you do, Dear?"
"I'd get a job and make some money."

A bright, spunky seventh grade girl gave me this report the other day, and I include it here to illustrate a point. If you haven't encountered this, you have at least met something just like it.

This, of course, is the reasoning not only of a concrete thinker but a thinker who expects the world to be just and logical. The two go hand in hand.

According to psychologists who stay awake at night and study such things, sometime between the age of twelve and fifteen we move from the world of concrete thinking where everything is reasonable and verifiable to a world of abstract thinking where we can make meaning from shades and hues and symbols. What the psychologists don't tell us is that we make this move kicking and screaming every step of the way. And why not? Just about the time we learn not to ask our parents "Why?" anymore, and we decide to live with not knowing why, someone comes along and tells us there is a whole other dimension to the world that we haven't even begun to see. It's a scary thought. And most middle schoolers protest it vehemently.

Let me illustrate. Most eighth graders don't like poetry just as a matter of principle. They tend not to trust people who walk barefoot through fields of daffodils. Later we discover that not many people like poetry, but eighth graders are the only ones honest enough to verbalize it. Imagine this scene in the eighth grade class as we paraphrase for brevity.

"Now, class, listen to the beauty of the poem. 'Little flower in the crannied wall, I pluck you out of the cranny, root and all. If I could understand who you are, then I would know who God and man is.' Oh, isn't that wonderful? Now tell me, class, what is the poet talking about when he speaks of a wall?"

Silence as the eighth graders glance at each other as if to say, "Our teacher has gone wacky."

"Come on, class, let's get into the spirit of the thing. What's the poet talking about when he talks of the wall?"

Finally, the brave class leader speaks. "He's talking about a wall."

"Well, not exactly. You see, sometimes a poet uses one word when he means something else."

"Well, that's bad writing. Why can't he just say what he means?"

And the teacher cries while wondering why no one in college ever told her about eighth graders who hang onto the concrete world as long as they can with all sorts of protests about moving into a world of symbols and abstractions.

But there is another characteristic here at work as well. Not only is the world supposed to be real and concrete, but it should be just and honest as well. It is important for all of us who have any kind of influence on children this age to keep this in mind. They expect their heroes to tell the simple, concrete truth; and they expect all questions to have specific answers. If we expect to be much of a positive role model, it's important for us to live our lives in such a way as to demonstrate precisely what we say we believe. Any variation from this could be dangerous and consequential.

In short, when we are around people this age, it's important for us to be who we say we are, and it's even important for us to be who they think we are.

If one of your middle schooler's role models such as a Sunday School teacher, a sports idol, or a parent slips up, that young person is going to have a rough time putting it all together. If you understand this, you are in a better position to offer explanation and counsel.

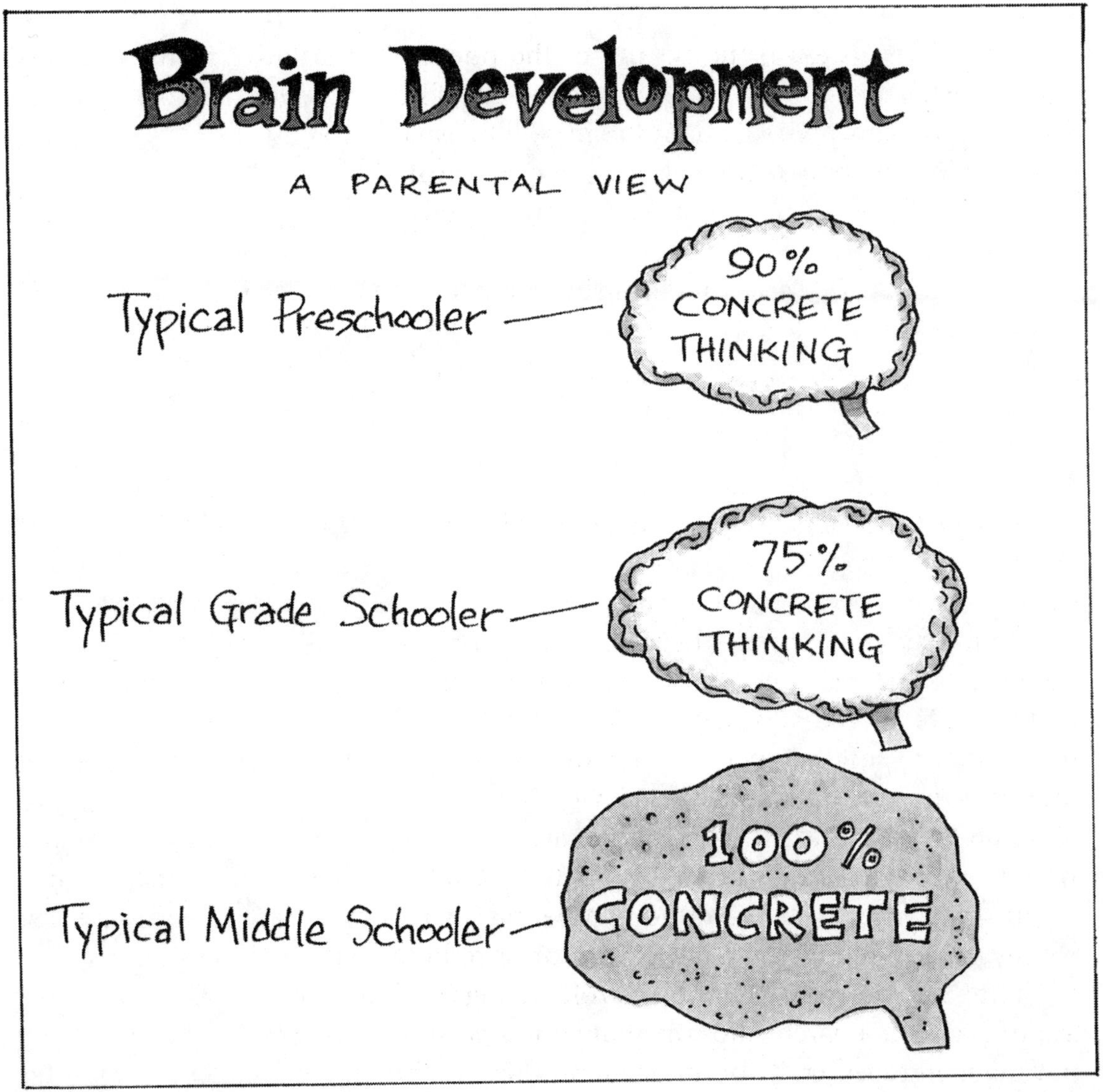
Brain Development
A PARENTAL VIEW
Typical Preschooler
90% CONCRETE THINKING
Typical Grade Schooler
75% CONCRETE THINKING
Typical Middle Schooler
100% CONCRETE

A few months ago, he was an innocent little boy
with pockets full of snails and puppy dog tails,
but now he can't even come to the dinner table without
combing his hair for at least thirty minutes.

Have you not heard about the TV cameras? When a person turns thirteen, these giant television cameras from up above come on and lock right on these people so that their every action of every second of the day is broadcast throughout the world filled with people who have absolutely nothing else to do but to sit and watch. If the whole world were watching you, you would be conscious of your hair too.

This phenomenon is called egocentrism. It may sound a bit unreasonable, but it is a haunting and disturbing reality. These people have decided in their own minds that everybody is watching them, and it won't do you much good to try to convince them otherwise.

So what do we do about it? We live with it. We know they are going to go through a period of egocentrism. They are going to be overconscious of the way they look—an unexpected zit is a disease serious enough to require quarantine. They are going to overreact to anything anyone says to them. They are going to be humiliated, embarrassed, and mortified at least once an hour. And they are going to live through it.

Perhaps our best response is to take it very seriously when we are with them and laugh about it when we are not.

I once heard a wise person explain the sequence of egocentrism. "When I was fourteen, I wanted to know what everyone was saying about me. When I turned twenty-four I didn't care anymore what they were saying. When I turned forty, I realized they weren't talking about me in the first place."

The middle school youth group has just spent the last week in church camp, and they make their report during Sunday evening service.

"It rained every day. We tipped the canoe over and almost drowned. We short-sheeted the counselor's bed. We had Bible study at night. We loved everybody, and I've never been so close to God in all my life. Thank you."

This is my favorite Sunday night of the year. I love these youth camp reports. I like the honesty and brevity, but I especially enjoy hearing them tell us so much about themselves.

These people are concrete thinkers. The psychology books say that they are supposed to move into abstract thinking very soon now, but middle schoolers don't read psychology books, so they give us the concrete thinker's report.

For them, Christianity is real. It is something you can see and touch and you can definitely feel. They don't get too much out of religiousese or sermonology. What they know is whether they felt something or not, and if they felt good, it must have been from God.

Isn't this a refreshing approach to the Christian experience? It reminds me of various Bible characters. Christ gave sight to the blind man. This man didn't know all the theology of what happened, but he just went around telling everybody that he could see, and that Jesus had done it. I see the middle schooler in this story. He doesn't know why he had fun at camp, but he did, and Jesus was the reason.

But this approach also carries a strong message to all of us—parents, teachers, and ministers alike. Because this is what being a Christian means to them, they expect to be able to see Christianity in the rest of us, particularly those of us who would presume to teach them about Christ.

If Christ and the teachings of Christ are real in our lives, middle schoolers should be able to see some visible evidence of that. They should see some happiness, some excitement, and a strong commitment to live by the moral code that they attach to being a Christian. Anything less than this can cause them serious concerns and maybe even damage.

When we choose their religious teachers, we should consider several qualities, but we must always keep in mind that young adolescents learn more from watching than from listening. Some of the best youth speakers I have ever seen are calm, gentle people who speak softly but honestly. Some of the best middle school teachers I have ever seen are calm, gentle people who speak softly but firmly and consistently day in and day out.

Middle schoolers are brighter than we often give them credit. They can spot a phoney. And they put far more importance on the visible results of a love for God than they do on the language that describes a love for God.

*"I hate you! I hate this family. I just want to leave."
And with that she does the next best thing. She runs
into her room and slams the door with finality. Thirty
minutes later, she pops back out all smiles and manners
and asks, "What's for dinner?"*

Who needs to go to the theme park to ride the roller coaster when you have a middle schooler in the house? When the body begins to fill up with strange new juices, when they live life in the whirlwind of flux, they have little alternative except to ride that emotional roller coaster.

Be comforted. This, too, is normal. It happens in the best of homes. It happens in the best of classrooms where favorite teachers can only look on in amazement. It even happens in peer groups.

For some reason, this never makes the Christmas newsletter. "Joe got a big promotion. We recarpeted the living room; and Heather spent the year on an emotional roller coaster." It's not the kind of thing we go door to door broadcasting, but it does happen.

I have always suspected that this instant and immediate display of the full range of emotions has something to do with experimentation. Hers is a world of change. Her body is changing. Her friendship pattern is changing. Her way of thinking about the world is changing. Her school environment is changing.

But the problem is that she doesn't like change any better than we do. To learn to live in this world of change, she experiments. Let me say that again with emphasis. Middle schoolers have to experiment. Because they are somewhere in a never-never land between childhood and adulthood, they have to experiment with what they think adults do. Because they are in the process of forming new friends, they have to experiment with the different kinds of behavior that these friendships would require. Because they really don't know how they feel about most of life, they have to experiment with emotions.

And your daughter is busy experimenting. She tried liking you, and that emotion didn't accomplish what she needed at that time. So she tries hating you. She can't just try hating you. She has to let you know that she hates you. She just can't leave the experiment up to you to decipher on your own. She has to assure you that at this particular moment she is all wrapped up in her hatred for you.

When she finds out that hatred isn't the right emotion—when she doesn't like herself while she is hating or when it doesn't achieve what she hoped it would, she tries love again. And all in a matter of minutes. To paraphrase an old weather report, "If you don't like your middle schooler, just wait a minute."

Actually, your daughter's display of hatred described here is rather mild. Most try to demonstrate their hatred with a bit more zest. I teach college seniors. These are people who have grown up successfully and are on their way to becoming professionals and productive adults. Every semester I ask the class, "Tell us about the time you ran away from home." Then for the next forty-five minutes or so, we sit and listen to all the stories. Almost everyone has a story. Sometimes they were only gone a few minutes; sometimes a few hours; some even overnight; but many of them actually carried the experiment so far that they literally left home.

It's funny now, but I'm sure that when it happened, there were some frightened, angry, and guilt-ridden parents somewhere. It does happen.

Probably the best advice we can give ourselves is that we need to be consistent in the midst of all this. There is nothing to be gained by answering her hatred and her hate-filled remarks with angry retorts or our own version of hatred. We all agree on this, until she throws a temper tantrum. That's when we need to remind ourselves, "Stay cool, keep quiet, and be available when she is finished with her test run."

If you really want to develop a reasonable relationship with your middle schooler, try this test. The next time you're in a group, ask two questions: (1) How old was Mary when Jesus was born? (2) How old was your grandmother when she married? Now, let's ponder those answers.

My theologian friends delight in telling me that Mary was about fourteen years old when Christ was born. They also delight in telling me that one of the biggest problems in modern America is that children fourteen years old are having babies.

My friends tell me that Grandma, that glorious person full of chocolate chip cookies and love, that paragon of wisdom and life and mature counsel, married when she was seventeen.

Do you see the problem here? Let's suppose that you have a thirteen-year-old at your house. To make it specific, let's suppose that thirteen-year-old is a girl. When your grandmother was that age, she was looking at about four years of adolescence before she crossed over that significant threshold of natural growth and became a fully participating adult, taking her place in the progress of humanity. Your thirteen-year-old daughter is looking at a decade of adolescence, or at least that's what you're looking at for her through your dreams and expectations.

We are living in a period of great paradox. We don't much like childhood, so we are rushing people through that as quickly as we can. We are starting children in education at least a year, and sometimes two or three years, earlier than my generation gave up our freedom to be incarcerated in institutions called schools.

We have replaced childlike games with adult imitations called Little League.

The researchers tell us that nature has responded to this rush through childhood, and that American children are now entering puberty about six months earlier than they did a generation ago. But here's the paradox. We rush them through childhood into an endless adolescence.

When your child is about twelve years old, Nature comes along and says, "Look at you. You're an adult. You can reproduce. You can work. You can take responsibility for yourself."

Culture, which is another word for Mother, says, "Not so fast. You cannot do those things until you have graduated from high...col.... graduate school," and we have just told them to put their maturity on "hold" for about ten years.

Adolescence isn't really much of a natural period. It is something we have created, and now we have to learn to live with it. As you read this book, and more important, as you look at your child, don't forget this. Here is a person who is straining at the controls and reins, ready to burst out into life fully armored and prepared to take on whatever the world has to offer. Yet, because she happened to be born at this time and place, we have to keep some of the symbols of childhood in place for now and for a few years to come.

This is why you get unexpected answers and strange behavior. This is why it is so hard to understand middle schoolers. They don't understand themselves either.

It happened so fast. One day she was twelve years old—a little girl with little girl charm. Two months later she turned thirteen, and all of a sudden, she looks eighteen. Wow!

Nature is cruel, and this is one of the cruelest tricks of all. You knew she was going to have that growth spurt. That is just one of the realities of the age, but you just can't prepare yourself for how quickly and how radically it comes. Why can't they just stay young and sweet for a while longer?

But as you have observed, this growth spurt is about much more than just physical appearance. As we mentioned earlier, in Luke 2:52, the biblical writer tells us that Jesus grew in stature, in wisdom, and in favor with God and man. In other words, normal growth comes in four categories—physical, intellectual, social, and religious. Your daughter's physical change is a reminder that a lot of other growth is going on as well.

But the problem comes when they don't grow in all those categories at the same speed and at the same time. At thirteen she looks eighteen, but you must remember that she is thirteen. It is important for you to remember that she is thirteen because some other people in her life are going to forget that. The boys in the neighborhood or in the youth group are going to lose sight of it—that's for sure. They have always considered her just another little kid; now they see her as an attractive peer and that's dangerous.

Some of her teachers will forget that she is only thirteen. Despite how many people teachers see and know, they still put expectations on the mature looking student that they don't put on the less mature looking one. If the teacher needs someone to go to the office to pick up forms, he will probably choose your daughter, just because she looks a little older than her peers.

This all may seem a bit flattering at first, but you need to remember that while your daughter had a physical growth spurt, she didn't have the same kind of emotional growth spurt. She may look eighteen years old, but emotionally, she's still thirteen, and she has to go through being thirteen before she turns eighteen. In other words, your daughter could well encounter some emotional challenges which she simply is not old enough to handle, and you are going to have to help her cope. Although she looks more like a woman than a little girl, it's all right for her to play with dolls, talk on the phone for hours, sleep with a teddy bear, want you to read her a story at night, and cry because she doesn't have any friends. A few weeks ago she was twelve years old. Don't lose sight of that.

Sometimes we adults get fooled because of their intellectual growth. Middle schoolers of today have been around more than the junior highers of my generation; they have either been there, done that, or seen it on television, and they know much more about the world than we did at their age. But they are still just as close to childhood as we were. They may see the more sophisticated side of life, but they still don't have the emotions to deal with it any better than we did.

Growth is a funny thing. It comes in spurts, but it doesn't all come at the same speed.

***On a skateboard, he is poetry in motion,
but he can trip and fall on his face just
walking across the floor.***

Even the body is a contradiction. Everything grows so fast that just to get it all under control is a major challenge. The hands, the feet, the arms, the legs, the mouth, and the hair all run amuck, and they don't know why.

I have never understood how early adolescents can master a complicated physical activity and then look so clumsy in the simple ones, but it happens. We need to be thankful for the complicated activities. They don't just skateboard. They do all those daredevil moves on the thing. They don't just ride a bicycle; they develop a whole routine of intricate bicycle tricks. They don't just play video games; they master video games and work their fingers with precision and fine dexterity.

But this is good. At the age when walking and chewing gum at once is a major challenge, it's good that they have an opportunity to develop intricate physical skills. Not long ago, I talked with a high school student who had masterfully manipulated his automobile to avoid a serious accident. He attributed his quick reflexes to having played hours and hours of video games. And we thought those were a curse!

But now that we have looked at the positive, we need to consider the other side. Having a squeaky voice and arms and legs which don't mind is not a laughing matter. When he falls walking across the room, you are baffled but amused. He is embarrassed. No wonder he is so self-conscious. He has to sit around and wonder,

When and where is the next dumb thing I'm going to do? These thoughts would cause any-one to be a bit self-centered. Your son doesn't enjoy being the comic relief of the family, so he builds defenses against it.

Growth is risky business, and our children learn how to handle it by trial and error. They catch up with their growth spurt by experimenting. That's why you see them sprawled out in church or always flailing around with arms and legs, just try-ing to discover their new potential and to get control of it all.

They also have to worry some about the permanence of the condition. We know that it's temporary, but they don't.

In the meantime, we need to give them all the support and encouragement we can for their participation in those specialized physical activities. We stifle our snickers when they fall, and we dream of the time in a not-so-distant future when we're old and decrepit and they will have to help us cross the street.

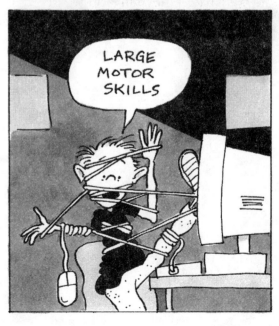

You were a fair baseball player, and you think he may be a chip off the old block. But when you propose that he try out for the team, he says, "I don't like baseball. It's a dumb game."

There's a small chance that he's telling the truth. But more than likely, he's scared to death. People this age spend most of their days being scared to death. That old monster of insecurity may well explain most of their strange behavior and obnoxious ways. It is the disease of the age. I rarely meet a middle schooler who likes himself or herself. There is always something wrong and someone better.

This is not always immediately obvious because insecurity never looks like insecurity. It always looks like something else. Sometimes insecurity comes in the form of arrogance and assurance, under the cloak of cool. Sometimes insecurity comes in the form of rudeness. Frequently, the middle school bully is the most insecure kid in the school. Often insecurity comes in the form of apathy. "That's dumb. I'm not going to try" can be translated as, "I'm scared to death that I can't do it, and I don't want to make a fool out of myself."

This seems to be where your son is; and even if you don't persuade him to go out for the baseball team, at least you've learned something very important about him. He often feels insecure and when he does, he sounds apathetic.

There are two ways to attack this frequently debilitating feeling of insecurity. We can attempt to build our children up by explaining to them that they are special, created by God with specific talents to be used for specific reasons. We can support this approach with frequent affirmations and kudos.

Or we can let them discover that they are capable by letting them prove to themselves that they are better than some others. If your son does go out for baseball and becomes an all-star, he will at least begin to feel more secure about his baseball playing because he knows he is better than someone else.

But how do we give middle schoolers an opportunity to try without running the risk of serious failure and deeper feelings of insecurity? That's a good question. In your son's case, you may want to take him out in the backyard and check out his skills to make sure he does have the talent to put himself on the line. Just to force him out for the team without his having some insight into the game and how he fits would be a serious mistake. On the other hand, if he does have the talent to succeed enough to enjoy baseball and he doesn't go out, then he will have cheated himself out of a boyhood experience that would have lasted a lifetime.

When I think of these situations, I'm often reminded of a young man who tried out for his high school basketball team but was cut. He persisted until he made a few teams and eventually wound up on a professional team—he was Michael Jordan. I wonder if he cried that night and told his parents, "I hate basketball, anyway. It's a dumb game."

"I don't know why I have to make my bed.
I'm only going to get back in it in twelve hours."

Isn't it wonderful? At twelve years of age he has completed his degree and is prepared to turn every issue of life into a debate topic.

Actually, he has been doing this since he was three and learned to say, "Why?" But in those day, we either lied to him or answered, "Because." Now our lies and "because" won't work. He has reached that age when he wants the world to be reasonable and logical, and when the world doesn't measure up to his expectations, he wants to know why.

"Why do I have to make my bed?"

"Why do I have to do the homework when I can work the problems already?"

"Why do you vote for politicians when you know they are going to break their promises?"

"Why do I have to take two plates to the kitchen sink when my sister only has to take one?"

Now admit it. Those are good questions. Forget for a moment that they come fast and furiously at the most inopportune moments and with various degrees of inflection.

Aren't you proud of him for practicing his skills of logic? He is growing into a thinking person. He is at least beginning to use his mind. This is a significant moment in his development and in your relationship.

In respect for his thinking and his questions, you attempt reasonable, studied, and thoughtful answers; and he evaluates your insightful responses with one simple judgment: "That isn't fair."

This little sentence is the key to understanding early adolescents and understanding our role as parents. They want life to be fair. They expect life to be fair. It is at this point that we realize what we as adults know that they don't know. It is a terrible lesson, and we may even wish it weren't true, but it is. We have to face it. Life is not fair. It never was, and it never will be.

Through the years we have learned that lesson, and we have learned to live in an unfair world. But how do you communicate that to a twelve-year-old Socrates?

When you are looking for ways to reason with a middle schooler, you have to begin with that one difference between them and us. They still think life should be fair.

Unfortunately, as they live a little longer, they come to realize that it isn't true and that we were right all along. But that is a danger, too, because at this point, they may become cynical and lose interest in even searching for the truth. That is why we as parents must teach and teach with great seriousness a two-pronged lesson—life isn't fair, but it is still good.

And we have to demonstrate that goodness even on those days when their bed isn't made.

"Six years ago last Tuesday, you promised me that if the Cubs ever got into the playoffs we would go. Well, the Cubs are in and we have to go."

They can't remember to close the refrigerator door or take the trash out. They can't remember to tell you about an important school meeting until about thirty minutes before it happens. They can't remember who called you on the phone. They can't remember the capital of Missouri for the test on Friday.

But middle schoolers are not brain dead!

They do remember the names, numbers, batting averages, and hometown of every player in the National League. They remember all the lyrics from each of the current top forty songs. They remember the telephone numbers of their eleven best friends. They remember combinations for three locks. And they remember every promise you ever made to them. This is good news? This is what we call selective memory.

Actually, there might be a little deception involved. When it comes to promises, have you noticed that they remember your saying things that you don't remember saying? For one thing, they listen with literal ears. You say, "This would be a good year to go to Disney World," and their ears pick it up, toss it around through all hearing mechanisms, get it entwined with all the other thoughts in their heads, and it comes into their brains as, "We're going to Disney World this year."

But this too is just one more clue into understanding how they reason. They are literal thinkers and they expect everyone else to be literal. Don't spice up your speech with abstract illustrations or embellishing phrases. Just give it to them straight. The more literally you say it, the more accurately they will hear it.

The other rather scary thought here is that they expect you to keep your promises. In the world they live in, which is filled with change and inconsistency and contradictions, they are searching for one person that is reliable, one person who means what he or she says and carries through on promises. They have chosen you to represent that stability, and they aren't reluctant to remind you of what they expect.

If you don't want to get caught in this, watch what you say and avoid making promises.

Or hire a lawyer.

***When he's in his room the noise he calls music
is so loud, you fear structural damage to the house.
When he's not in his room, he's got a permanent
set of walkman headphones around his ears.***

As long as there is music, there will be a generation gap, and parents and children will have something to fight about.

The first conclusion we draw from the current music mania is the role noise plays in the lives of young adolescents. It seems that noise is necessary for them to verify their existence. Descartes said, "I think; therefore I am." The teenager says, "My ears are ringing; therefore I am."

Notice them when they get too far away from noise and stay too long. They suffer either from a serious identity crisis or withdrawal pains, but they definitely suffer. Have you observed that even when they are watching television, they have to have some background noise? How they concentrate on their homework with that music blaring defies any kind of scientific research and learning theory.

The next issue to consider is the changing criteria of music appreciation. Gone are the days when we listened for such things as harmony, texture, or perhaps even poetry. Now, the essential quality of good music is that it is loud. Rare among us are those old enough to remember when music was not an electronic media blessed with many decibels.

Now that we have all agreed on these issues, we have to admit that this conflict is ageless. Parents and children have been fighting over their tastes in music for centuries. There isn't anything new here.

But this is good. Each generation carves out its own identity and records its special place in the march of time with a distinct quality in music. That stuff blaring from that walkman or stereo represents your son's special moment in history. The songs don't sound like the songs of your generation, but those will be the songs he will listen to when he is forty and tunes into the golden oldies station. (That's a sobering thought.) No doubt these songs will remind him of an earlier period when the world was simpler and purer and boyhood was glorious.

Each generation needs its identity—its special memories and its art. Kennedy's assassination; the night the Beatles appeared on Sullivan; the coming of disco; the Challenger explosion; and Pat Boone singing "Love Letters in the Sand"—these are all memories which unite us to that segment of the population we call "our generation."

What about those reports that some of the current music is morally bankrupt and playing it too loud can even be physically impairing? I think we should take those reports seriously and acquaint ourselves with what our children are actually listening to and how they are playing it. If this requires slipping off to watch MTV, then we need to do it.

As a parent, you have a right and even the responsibility to set some rules for life, and this includes your son's choice in music. Don't be afraid of this, but as you do make your decision, keep in mind the ageless conflict and what his reasons are for his music.

I find it refreshing to remember that my parents survived the jitterbug; my generation survived Elvis; your generation survived The Grateful Dead, and there is a good chance that your son is going to make it through Rap. Can you imagine a time in the future when these rap stars of today come on TV and seem as innocent as the rerun of an old Elvis movie does now?

"Mother, will you help me so I can do this by myself!"

The old independent/dependent paradox raises its head one more time. But you should be ready for it by now. It's been going on all her life. You taught her how to tie her shoes, but then she wouldn't let you hug her. She went to school and learned to read, but then she wouldn't sit on your lap for a while.

Now that she's entered middle school, this conflict has become acute. She so wants to be independent. She looks at her body, and it tells her she is grown up. When you admonish her, you often say, "You're too old for that kind of behavior." She hears of people her age who are already half into life. And she just needs to know what independence feels like.

Some transitions in our lives come gradually. We move from one stage to another over a long enough period of time that we don't even realize we are moving.

Some transitions come abruptly. For example, one moment we're not married; the next moment we are. Moving into independence is one of the transitions that too often comes abruptly. While she is in middle school and high school, someone is always telling her exactly what to do—when to go to bed, when to get up, what to eat, when to study, when to watch TV, what music to listen to, what to believe, and what to think. In the midst of all this, she cries out for any form of independence she can find. It may seem as if she is being rebellious, but I think that she is experimenting—just trying to get some sense of what being independent really is and whether she can handle it when it comes.

Too often we don't help much in her search for independence until one specific day when, suddenly, we bombard with the whole measure. Frightening, isn't it?

Because this abrupt move into independence comes at different times for different people, it is difficult to set an exact moment for the shock, but entering college serves as one example. Just to illustrate that, consider that researchers tell us that many college freshmen gain fifteen pounds that first year. Once they escape the rigors and rules of home meals and enter into eating independence, they don't have the discipline to avoid the junk food. In other words, they aren't prepared for their new-found independence.

Having a child grow into middle school age is a reminder that we need to change some of the characteristics of our relationship with her. It is time for us to begin to let her explore life on her own a bit more, and change some of the rules. It's time to love her enough to turn her loose.

One of the manifestations of love is trust, and trust means that we give them more room and more freedom. Letting go is surely one of the hardest tasks of parenthood.

PART 4

School

*She was always a good math student, so she qualified for pre-algebra in the eighth grade. She worked hard the first nine weeks and made an **A**. But all of a sudden, things changed. She quit studying, and her grade has dropped out of sight.*

I know the answer to this. I spent many years of my life as a teacher and a parent not knowing the answer to it; and I misjudged and mistreated many students until I learned. I still wake up with nightmares of images of this girl.

She isn't lazy or defiant or even in a math block. She just missed a point. It's that simple, and it happens every day. Classes like math, foreign language, science, and maybe everything else are based on a series of sequential concepts. She masters today's concept, and then she is ready for tomorrow's concept. It's a simple building process.

But the problem comes when, for some reason, your daughter doesn't master today's concept. Perhaps she was absent; perhaps she just wasn't paying attention; perhaps the teacher didn't explain it clearly. But for some reason, she missed one concept.

The following day, she is lost. She doesn't understand. The lesson just doesn't make any sense without the concept she missed. To make it even worse, the rest of the class seems to understand, so your daughter tells herself that she's stupid and can't learn it, which she can't without that one missing concept.

The teacher, if she is good, sees the confusion and tries to help. She asks, "What is it you don't understand?" Have you ever tried to analyze that question? Better yet, have you ever tried to answer it? If you knew what it was you didn't understand and you could explain it to someone, you would probably understand what you don't understand.

At this point, your daughter and every other student I've ever seen quits. She begins to hate math. She hates the book, the class, the teacher, and the homework, all because she missed one concept.

I have a thousand illustrations of this. The kindergarten student included a little fat figure into her drawing of the nativity scene. When the teacher asked for clarification, the bright young student reported, "That's Round John Virgin."

For most of my life, I have believed that the Philippines were in the Caribbean. Ten years ago, I learned that they aren't, but I also learned why I have been wrong. The only time I ever studied the Philippines was in conjunction with the Spanish–American war.

See how it happens? It comes so innocently and so quickly that we don't even know that we have lost the concept.

So what do you do with your daughter? I don't know the technique, but there has to be some way for you to climb into her mind and find out which concept is not there. If you're good in math yourself, maybe you could do it by just helping her work some of the problems. If you're not that good, think seriously of getting a good tutor, and explain to the tutor what the problem is before you even start.

Whatever you do, you need to give her help and do it quickly. This is a solvable problem if you catch it soon enough and tackle it in the right way.

You bought her the largest backpack you could find, but she still complains that it isn't large enough.

L et's look at her day for a moment. During the first hour, she has English. For English class she needs to bring two pens—a blue one and a red one each day. On Monday, Wednesday, and Friday, she is to bring her grammar book. On Tuesday, Thursday, and Friday, she is to bring her literature book. On Monday and Wednesday, she is to bring her spelling book. On Tuesday and Friday, she is to bring her vocab book. On Monday, Wednesday, and Thursday, she is to bring her journal notebook. On Tuesday and Wednesday, she is to bring her official notebook. On Wednesday and Friday, she is to bring her composition notebook. And every other Friday, she is to bring a free reading book.

During second period, she has math, and we go through it all over again.

To make matters worse, there is no time to go to the locker. In many schools, she is only allowed to go to her locker twice a day. So the solution is to carry it all with her every day.

You can be comforted. She probably isn't dealing in contraband, and she isn't stealing large items from somewhere. She is simply surviving with the conditions at hand, and that larger backpack seems rather necessary.

How she's going to carry it is another problem which we will leave up to her. Not long ago, I watched a seventh grade student stand at her locker and prepare her backpack for the day. You could tell from the expressions on her face and some hesitancy that she was thinking through her day's requirements carefully, choosing just those absolutely essential items. But when she finally got everything in and was satisfied that she had covered all the bases, she couldn't lift the backpack.

At that point, she became a higher order thinker and a problem solver. She got down on her hands and knees, put the pack on her shoulder, crawled to the wall, pulled herself up, and ran down the hall into the happy–go–lucky life of a typical seventh grader.

No wonder they have bad posture and precise memories.

He always had to work hard in elementary school,
but now that he's entered middle school
as a sixth grader, his life is a catastrophe.

This is the perfect example of the student I worry most about. The reason he struggled in elementary school was that he was a bit behind his peers in the development of learning skills such as reading, writing, and doing basic arithmetic. We have no way of knowing for sure why he was behind. Maybe he missed crucial days in the early grades and failed to pick up a concept. Maybe his God-given gifts just don't include skill with language and math. Maybe he just takes a little longer to think through the task.

Regardless of the reason for his struggles, he made it; but he made it because he had help and because he had focus. Elementary school is about developing learning skills. You learn to read, to write, and to do arithmetic.

Middle school is about using learning skills to learn other material. Instead of learning to read, he uses his reading skills to learn social studies and science and English. If he goes to middle school without full mastery of those learning skills, he ends up struggling as your son is now.

Let's understand his plight. He isn't lazy or unmotivated or dumb. In all probability, he is working harder than most of his peers but with less positive reinforcement. In short, he's suffering on both ends—hard work and no reward.

This is a classic sign, and your son needs help. He needs to get on top of those skills. In other words, he needs to get more comfortable with the skills before he is asked to use the skills to master the other material. Now is the time to act. To delay is only to add to his frustration until he does become unmotivated and chooses to fail.

You have two options, and neither is a guarantee. You could attempt to get him some tutoring. Some private clinics do excellent work with some students just like your son. I've been involved in some of these where we have almost unbelievable success stories. In just a few sessions, the student identifies his problem, whips it, and goes on to academic success. But on the other hand, we have less than successful stories too. You have to assess each case on its own merit.

The other possibility is a more sobering one. If your son is behind in developing skills, you may want to give him a chance to catch up. In other words, you may want him to take sixth grade again.

I realize how painful this possibility is, and I realize that it, too, is a gamble. I've seen students who have done this and handled it quite effectively, but I've also seen the opposite. You must consider your son and his case.

He will, of course, profit from the additional year of repeating the skills, but what will all this cost him in social adjustment? How strong are his friendships? How mature is he in relationship to his peers? Can you send him to another school where he can just start over in his social relationships?

These are the questions you need to ask.

***Now that he's in seventh grade, he comes
home after school every day and sleeps two hours.***

I know that this causes us concern, but there may be a good, simple reason for this. Maybe he's tired. Because we don't have any evidence to begin to think otherwise, let's start there.

A day in seventh grade is tough, and it would wear me out. A few years ago, someone wrote a book about the transitions we go through in our lifetime and the psychological and physical strain those put on us. One of the biggest transitions of life was left out of the book, and that is the year that we move from a self-contained classroom into a departmentalized school. In other words, we move from being with one teacher in one room with one group of classmates for six hours a day to being with seven different teachers and hundreds of different classmates each day.

Some students enjoy the change and variety. Some get lost and disoriented; but all of them have to make serious adjustments in both the emotional and physical world.

This is where your son is. He's trying to figure out a new building. He is trying to discover quick routes from class to class. He's trying to adapt to seven new sets of teacher rules. Just trying to remember where he sits in each class is a drain. He's trying to learn the names of some of his classmates, and to top it all off, he probably has three combination locks in his life.

No wonder he's tired. The only way that your son can make it through the school day right now is to pump adrenaline. He needs it to travel the halls, to stay awake in class, and to manage the new social challenges.

When he gets home and the adrenaline drains out, he crashes. It's not only a healthy response to his day, but it is probably the only response.

Right now, your son needs you as badly as he ever has needed you in his life. Try to find out what's going on in his day. You can't do anything to make it any easier, but at least you can show him that you care and that you are trying to understand. This in itself is the most positive thing you can contribute to his adjusting to the transition he has had thrust upon him.

In the meantime, let him sleep.

Your eighth grade daughter asks for help with her homework, and you discover it is something you studied during college.

Of course it is, and if you think about it, you shouldn't be too surprised. This has been going on ever since she started school. In kindergarten, she learned what we learned in second grade. In fourth grade, she learned what we learned in eighth grade. Now that she is in eighth grade, she is ready to cover what we learned in college.

It seems that most of us are caught in something of a dilemma. On one hand, we hear stories about how inadequate the American schools are, but on the other hand, we see our own children studying material three to five years ahead of when we studied it.

I am not going to attempt to reconcile this dilemma, but I do want to emphasize that understanding this is important to our reasoning with our children. For starters, think about how long your daughter has been in intense academic endeavor. Most of our generation attended a kindergarten which was predominantly playing and sharing. Your daughter attended a kindergarten which was probably far more academically rigorous. Now that she is in the eighth grade, we can ascertain that she has spent at least a year longer in formal education than we did. If she went to any kind of preschool, make that two years. If you catch your daughter taking a bit of an academic breather, it could be that she has worn herself out. Don't despair. This, too, is normal.

Another factor to be considered in this hurry-up schedule is something I shall call age appropriateness. What is the proper age to learn calculus? Or does it matter? What is the proper age to read *The Scarlet Letter*? Or does it matter?

I am not raising this issue in an attempt to reform the educational system. My motive is altogether different. We are talking about understanding and reasoning with your eighth grader. Well, this is one of the factors you have to consider when you try to ponder what is going on during her day. If your daughter is making satisfactory grades and has good attendance, she is working hard in school. She is meeting hundreds of new ideas each week. She is covering material that you didn't even know about until you were about four years older than she.

Maybe this will help to explain some of her frustrations and outbursts.

***Your eighth grade daughter has three hours
of homework every night, so much that you
can't even have much family life.
How much is enough?***

Wow, this is tough, and I don't have any kind of satisfactory answer. I hear it all the time, and I suspect that it has to do with a general confusion in this country about the status of education. National statistics tell us that the average student has forty minutes of homework a week. Teachers hear this statistic and decide to take action and do their part. So they give homework, and your daughter has no family life. It is a dismal circle of events.

The problem is that we haven't realized that different students take different approaches to homework responsibility. For purpose of clarity, let's divide students into three categories. First, we have the *conscientious ones*. Apparently, your daughter falls into this group. When these people have an assignment, they do it. They do it all. Many of them do more than is required. They look up words; they read the whole assignment; they take notes; and all that takes three hours every night.

But then we have the *shortcutters*. They do the homework, but they have learned to take shortcuts and get by. Instead of spelling words correctly, they write sloppily. On reading assignments, they hit the high spots and topic sentences; and they finish in about an hour.

Finally, we also have the students who *don't do the homework*. They just ignore the assignment and take the consequences.

Someone with a sharp pencil and good math skills averages all this together and comes up with forty minutes of homework a week. The nation gets upset; teachers get defensive; and conscientious students get overburdened.

I have mixed feelings about homework. Some is necessary, I agree; but my test of too much depends on what the teachers do with it. If the teachers don't read and make comments on every piece of work within a short period after it is submitted, then that's too much. As a parent, I get disturbed. Family life is far more important than busy work.

I do have suggestions for you. (1) Make sure the teachers know how long your daughter is spending on homework. Your daughter has five to eight teachers who never talk to each other. They have no idea how much homework the other teachers are assigning. Don't be shy. Tell them. (2) Convince your daughter that it is not failure to accept less than her best on every assignment. (3) Build in some relaxation for your daughter. With a schedule like this, she will wear herself out before she finishes school. One of the lessons she needs to learn is how to pace herself.

**He brings home a solid report card—all B's.
As a matter of curiosity, you ask,
"How many in your class made A's?"**

**He starts to cry, runs into his room,
and doesn't come out all evening.**

O ne of the baffling mysteries of life is the difference between perception and reality. You know what you said, and you know the implications behind it. In your reality, you were as innocent as you could ever be.

Obviously, that isn't how he perceived it. He perceived your open criticism, your rejection of his success, and your overt pressure for him to do better. When he relates this to his friends, you will come off as one of the leading ogres in the history of mankind. "I work my tail off to bring home B's, and my mom yelled at me because I didn't do better. What does she want from me? I'm tired of her always yelling at me and putting pressure on me because of my grades."

I hear these reports every day. One day one of my students just started crying in class for no apparent reason. When I asked, she told me what had happened the night before. She had been swimming in the pool when her father came by and asked, "How many laps tonight?"

"Ten," she answered.

"Well, you'll never get into the Olympics on ten laps a night," he said and went about his business. It sounded rather innocent to me and maybe even a bit clever —one father's stab at humor. But when I tried to explain that to the student, twenty-seven eighth grade lawyers took her side and argued me down.

"No," they yelled in one voice. "That's the way parents do it. Always putting pressure on us to be what we're not."

Okay, so this is how they perceive it. What's the harm? Over more than thirty-five years of helping other people rear their children, the one thing I've come to know for sure is that the worst sin parents can commit is to put expectations on their children which the children can't fulfill. I see this every day too, in a variety of manifestations—grades, sports, music, or even socialization. Even if parents don't intend to put on these pressures, the children perceive it that way; and they live with feelings of insecurity, failure, and futility.

But now that I've said that, let me nominate my idea for the second biggest sin parents can commit—not putting enough pressure on their children and letting them waste their God-given talents.

Wouldn't it be wonderful if children came with their degree of abilities and gifts stamped on their foreheads? Then we would know, and parenting could become an exact science. But it isn't stamped anywhere, and regardless of how much we want to, we can't climb inside them to determine what they are capable of doing. So we live with the age-old method of trial and error and a little guilt when they run into their bedroom and cry all night because of some innocent little comment we made.

Your eighth grade son never has homework, but he has decent grades.

This is as much a matter of concern as having too much homework. It is just not usual for eighth graders not to have homework. You really should investigate.

There are three possibilities.

(1) Your son has homework, but he just isn't doing it. That doesn't seem too likely because he is keeping his grades in the satisfactory range. The problem with some eighth grade homework is how students define work. Most students don't consider a reading assignment as an assignment. If the teacher says, "Read the next chapter in the textbook," most eighth graders don't read anything. They simply assume that there is no need to read because the teacher is going to talk about it tomorrow anyway. Some read the headings, picture captions, and summaries. A few read every word. On the other hand, if the teacher says, "Outline the next chapter in the book," eighth graders believe that they have a homework assignment.

It is possible that your son is in several courses where teachers are giving reading assignments without requiring much written work, and your son has discovered how to take shortcuts.

(2) Your son has learned to use his time efficiently. Most teachers do give students time to work during class. Most students don't work during those times. They talk to their neighbors, catch a couple of winks, or prepare for the next class.

Perhaps your son is one of those very rare individuals who actually takes that time to do his homework. If he is bright, or if he works in cooperation with his peers, or if he consults the teacher on the rough spots, he will drastically minimize the time required; and he just may be getting almost all of his work completed during class.

If this is the case, celebrate. You have a fine son and a fine student on your hands. He has learned a big lesson which will carry him far as a student and in life.

(3) The teachers aren't assigning much homework. If this is true, you should be a little concerned. Of course, the opposite situation where the student has so much homework he can't take a shower at night isn't the coveted answer either. But eighth graders do need to do a bit of homework.

There are some ideas presented in class which simply need to be developed and applied in a more elaborate form. There are some ideas presented in class which need to be repeated and recited in some written form. There are some ideas presented in class which need to be discussed and analyzed with parents and other thoughtful adults.

All this implies homework. Applying, repeating, and analyzing are valuable—yea, necessary habits, for all students as they continue their education through high school and college.

In other words, your son needs to do some homework just for the sake of learning the discipline of doing some homework. If he doesn't learn how to do that now, he is going to struggle sometime in the future.

How do you know which of the three possibilities is most accurate? The answer is so obvious that you already know it.

You have to go see his teachers. You don't want to be defensive or critical, but you need to assure them that you want to know why he doesn't have homework. When you find the reason, then both you and the teachers will be in a position to decide the appropriate strategy from there.

He was a good student, but during eighth grade,
something happened. He just doesn't seem to care.
Sometimes he finishes his homework but doesn't even
take it to school to turn it in.

If you and I can explain this, we will become rich and famous.

Everyone knows what a motivated learner is, and teachers and parents alike would rather have a motivated learner than an unmotivated one. The problem is that we just don't know what causes middle schoolers to be motivated.

Your son's case is troublesome because he was once a good student but seems not to be motivated anymore. Let's guess at some of the possible reasons.

It could begin with his social development. Perhaps as an eighth grader, he has taken up membership with a group of students who don't believe in good grades. With the people he is trying to impress, it just isn't cool to be a good student, to participate in class, and to hand in homework. At this point, his membership and acceptance in the group is far more important than his grades, so he obeys the whims of his peers instead of the expectations and hopes of his teachers and parents.

Another possibility is that he has lost sight of his goal and the reason for all this study. As we have discussed in other places, he is in a period of searching for logic and reason. He wants life to be fair and the world to make sense. He carries this over to his studies. If he isn't planning to travel to Africa sometime in the near future, he sees no urgent need to spend the evening making a map of Africa.

Every learner comes to every learning situation with a burning question on his mind, "Why are we doing this?" If the learner finds an answer to that question in

THE MIDDLE SCHOOL MAZE **122**

realistic application, he will be motivated. If he doesn't find the answer, then he may not work too enthusiastically.

Some eighth graders have a very clear set of goals and know exactly where they are going. They, too, may not see the immediate worth of drawing a map of Africa. But if they see how this activity helps them achieve an educational goal, they stay up half the night and draw a map of Africa.

Another possible reason that your son has decided to take the year off academically is that he doesn't like his teachers. His indifference is his way of affirming his independence and expressing his unhappiness with his teachers. He just won't do the work, and that will teach them a lesson or two.

As you ponder these explanations, remember that they are only possibilities. Maybe one of them is the reason. Maybe in a strange way, they all figure in; or maybe none applies. But you do need to investigate. Don't ask your son. He probably does not know the answer himself. At the same time, don't accuse him of being lazy or dumb. These are probably not the reasons his grades have fallen off.

Consult his teachers. You may begin with his favorite teacher or at least the one he talks about most. But your research may demand that you meet with all of them. If you ask the school officials, they will arrange such a meeting for you. I've never gotten much out of meeting like this. Eight teachers sit across the table from two frightened parents. There just isn't that much worthwhile communication in such an encounter. Instead, if you really need some insight into your son's situation, meet those teachers individually—the more informally the better.

But there is one more warning. Don't let your son's interest in his school work come between the two of you. He is still a good guy even if he does have a *D* in math. Don't base your relationship with him on this. Whatever his reason for this new approach to school, he hasn't ruined his life or jeopardized his chances at success. Almost every successful adult I know once had a bad year in school. This, too, is typical and not terminal.

There is a parent meeting at your school to discuss whether you should have a middle school or a junior high school. You really want to be a concerned parent, but you aren't sure you know the difference.

Neither does anyone else. The definitions change depending on who's using them. Go to the meeting and ask all the questions you need to in order to get a full picture. The other parents there will appreciate you.

When junior highs were established about 1910, they were buildings that housed ninth graders, eighth graders, and seventh graders. The curriculum and methods of instruction were similar to those at the high school except scaled down a bit.

During the sixties, educators and other experts decided that people this age have special kinds of developmental and educational needs which weren't being met in traditional junior high schools, so the concept of the middle school was born.

Notice even the change in implication with the name. These are not scaled down versions of high schools. Middle schools are supposed to be a distinct type of educational institution designed to meet the peculiar developmental needs of students at a particular age.

With this new idea, the most obvious change was in the age grouping. The educators decided that there was a huge maturity gap between seventh graders and ninth graders, so they decided to move the ninth graders out of the building and up into the high school. In many places, they then moved sixth graders into the building so that there would still be three grade levels.

I think it is important for us to pause here and ponder this age grouping practice. Schools are struggling with it, but churches, club groups, and parents are struggling as well. What do you do with sixth graders at church? Do you move them into the youth group, or do you leave them in children's church? Are ninth graders emotionally mature enough to be grouped with high school seniors? These are significant questions which shouldn't be dismissed with merely convenient answers.

Most middle schools also have something of a different approach to class arrangement. Rather than having the students randomly select five or six courses from the smorgasbord called the curriculum, students in a particular grade level are divided into groups which are often called pods. The pods usually contain between 100 and 120 students who have most of their classes together. Four teachers—a science teacher, a social science teacher, a math teacher, and language arts teacher—are designated to teach a specific pod, and they form a team so they can plan the classes, discuss the students, and work together on common problems. With this arrangement, students have a bit of the same feel for their classes as they had in elementary school when they had one teacher and one group of classmates.

The other positive possibility from this arrangement is that the teachers can work together to provide some innovative learning techniques to accommodate special needs of specific students.

Another practice is to give these pods a catchy name so that students have some sense of belonging when they say, "I'm in Seven Blue" or "Eight Achievers."

Another popular idea is the concept of exploratory classes. The idea behind this is that people this age need to sample a wide variety of learning experiences in order to determine what their interests and God–given talents really are. Thus, they sample from a menu which might include a semester of foreign language, a semester of shop, a semester of music, and a semester of art.

Notice throughout this discussion, the use of words such as *most* and *usually*. There is no precise description of what a middle school is, and that's why you need to attend all the meetings you can.

He's small; he's fragile;
but he's pleading to try out
for the middle school football team.

Maybe he's heard an old song, "You have to be a football hero if you want to get along with the beautiful girls." Unfortunately, it is still truer than it should be. You can protest this as not right. You can even deny it if you want, but it is still the way things are.

In our middle schools and high schools, the athletes are the central figures and key players. The teachers know who they are. Other students know who they are. And they know who they are. They form friendships among themselves. They tell inside jokes; they sit together and burp in the cafeteria; and they hit each other on the arm. Your son wants to be a part of that.

There are surely other clubs which he could join where size and build would not be so crucial; but he doesn't want to be in those other clubs. He wants in the football club. You can try reasoning and persuasion, but you still won't cool his desire to be a part of all that macho stuff.

He has figured out that if he's going to be any kind of a noticeable person in school, he has to get involved in sports; and football is his choice.

So what's the harm? Your first thought is that he will get hurt. That is a real risk, but he isn't any more of a candidate to get hurt than any of the other players. The coaches know he is small. They won't intentionally mismatch him against people much bigger than he.

But, you argue, at his size, he has no chance of making the team. He may sit on the bench so much that he grows to it. That's all right too. For one thing, football is one sport where the coaches don't usually cut anyone from the squad. They at least let everybody hang around and practice. Your son doesn't have to get into the games to be a part of the team and to be someone important. Just showing up for practice is enough to earn the right to wear his jersey to class on game day, and that's what football is all about anyway.

The other possibility is that he may not always be small and fragile. He may grow up to become the high school star. It has happened in the past, and it will happen again. As spunky as he is, you may still be the parent of an all-American someday.

Undaunted by size, the Middle School
Chess Club was determined to try out for football.

On a whim, you decide to visit your daughter's middle school; and the first thing that catches your attention is a dog roaming the hall.

We run into harsh reminders of reality everywhere we turn. That dog is a strong statement of the kind of world your daughter lives in. There are drugs in that school. In fact, there are enough drugs that the school officials have decided that it is a problem severe enough to invest in a dog project.

We know about such a world. We read about it in the papers; we hear about it as we talk with friends. But we observe our own children—so young and innocent looking—and we just decide that it is a foreign world, another place and time. Then we see a dog in her school and come face-to-face with the fact that the reality is here.

There is a good possibility that the problem doesn't touch your daughter directly. The fact that she forgot to tell you about the dog is promising. Perhaps she just doesn't think about it. It's important for us parents to remind ourselves of this. School is a big place. It is filled with several hundred students. Your daughter knows only a very small number of them. There are places in the building which your daughter never visits. There are activities going on every day which she doesn't know anything about. There is a strong possibility that your daughter has never seen drugs, has never seen a drug transaction, and doesn't know anybody who is involved with the drugs. But the drugs are still there, and your daughter does live in that world.

The other issue in this is the dog. The school is dealing with the drug problem the best it knows how. It is taking action and has invested in the dog.

The dog is probably something of an inconvenience, at least to some. But for your daughter to go to a drug-free school, she will have to accept some inconvenience. That is just the way the world works. The presence of the dog probably won't stop those people who are taking drugs, but it will drive their activities somewhere else. They won't be able to bring their drugs to school, and they won't be able to sell them there. This is the good news for you and your daughter.

But this does lead all of us parents to a sobering warning. Our children live in a world where drugs are available. We could wish it were not so, but that doesn't make it so. Our children aren't immune. We can't hide our heads in the sand and hope the problem goes away. As parents we need to face it, and we need to give our support to the programs and the people who are dealing with the problem.

First, we need to know what those programs are, and we need to know what they cover. Most schools now have a regularly scheduled drug information program of some kind which is designed to tackle the problem of drug usage among children and adolescents. These go by different names, but D.A.R.E. is one of the most common. Ask your daughter about such a program. It is more important to hear her report than for you to ask school officials because you are interested in her perception instead of theirs. After you know what the program covers, you will know what you must do to supplement that instruction.

You do need to pay attention and supplement that instruction. There is no need to panic or lock middle schoolers in the closet, but you do need to pay attention by talking, listening, and observing. If you detect serious changes in personality, a complete upheaval in friendship, listlessness, or other kinds of prolonged unusual behavior, you may want to contact the counselors at school, the youth minister at your church, or someone else who can give you wise counsel and support.

Despite the seriousness and complexity of this problem, the biggest defense you still have is to send your daughter to bed every night assured that she is loved and accepted.

"I got a demerit in PE today. I didn't dress out because someone stole my sweat socks out of my locker."

Isn't it wonderful to see how responsible middle schoolers are? They never forget it, or misplace it, or lose it.

Isn't it terrible that they have to live in a world of petty thieves who can steal anything down to a pair of stinking sweat socks right out of a padlocked locker?

In thirty-six years of working with people this age, I've never had one lose anything. They are so good about keeping their possessions and knowing exactly where they left them and where they should be.

But I've always had a problem with those thieves who creep in and steal. Perhaps it's elves who have it out for them.

If I were your daughter, I would sue, and that's probably what she said she was going to do if she caught that lowdown piece of life who took her sweat socks. She remembers distinctly taking her socks off, folding them up, and putting them in the proper place in the locker. She has done it every day of the semester, and she is absolutely positive that she did it yesterday. There is not even the most remote possibility that she did anything else. Thus, the reason her sweat socks are not in her locker today is that someone stole them. And that's the true picture of the situation. Case closed.

Now, I would never accuse anyone of lying. I am sure she is telling you the truth

131

just as she remembers it to be. When she showed up at her locker this morning and discovered her socks missing, she played it over and over in her mind, and that is the way it played out; so that must be the truth.

The problem is that she is so convincing. She's convincing because she's convinced. This has something to do with the philosophical difference between perception and reality. Regardless of what actually happened, when she played it over in her mind, she came up with this picture, and she really is convinced that this is the truth.

The moral of this story is a simple one. Get a second opinion. Again, I'm not accusing her of lying, but young adolescents are so good at rewriting the truth that we need to move cautiously. There are always two sides to any incident. Check them both out before you make a decision.

This isn't the end of the world. It doesn't mean that she is a compulsive liar. You don't have to hang your head in shame for the gaps in her moral training.

Just get her a new pair of socks and try to remember that she sometimes colors reality a bit.

She decided to try out for a part in the spring musical. She was so excited. You could hear her practicing in her room way into the night.

Two days after the try-outs, they posted a list of the cast on the classroom door. She didn't get the part.

Nothing ventured; nothing gained."

"You never know what you can do until you try."

"If I had to live my life over again, the one thing I would do is take more risks."

The little clichés sound harmless enough until you try one of them. For all of us, life is a series of achievements and setbacks. As the years go by, we learn that to have the achievements, we have to have a few setbacks. That's the way it works, but it still doesn't erase the pain.

The degree of pain depends on the amount of emotion we spend seeing ourselves in the achievement circle. For her, not getting into the spring musical is one of the most severe blows she has ever encountered. No one casually tries out for the musical. No one casually tries out for cheerleader. No one casually tries out for a sports team.

Before she tried out, she tried on the emotion of being in the musical. She obviously liked that emotion, or she wouldn't have worked so hard to get there. Now, to be told that she isn't good enough to wear that emotion is one of the worst forms of rejection she can ever meet.

This is a critical moment for her and for you. Tonight is not going to be an easy night. She has met failure and rejection; and she hurts. Now, both of you have to respond in such a way that she isn't afraid to try again.

It's easy to say, "Well, you can always try next year." And you can even tell her stories of people who persisted until they succeeded at something. Despite your sermons and encouragement, the hurt lingers on.

Let me share a little trick of parenthood I've picked up through the years. Talking with her is good, but talk won't reach the pain which is too deep for that. She needs an achievement—a major accomplishment.

I recommend that you wait until this exact moment to take her out to the parking lot in the mall after hours and teach her how to drive the car. This is the perfect time. Don't worry about keeping her up late. She wasn't going to sleep much tonight anyway. You don't have to stay out until she is an accomplished motorist. Just save this moment to let her get behind the wheel and experience the sheer exhilaration of being in charge of that automobile.

You know you are going to have to do it someday. I am just suggesting that you pick the most opportune time.

Psychologists tell us that we achieve psychological health by accomplishing significant tasks along the way—tying our shoes, riding a bicycle, and learning to read. In our society, with our love affair with the automobile, learning to drive is high on that list. She will never forget the night she first began the adventure.

Tomorrow when she goes to school, she'll have to face the girl who got the coveted part, and that won't be easy. But it will help some if your daughter can smile and say under her breath, "Well, at least, I know how to drive."

Postscript

Mom, I'm sorry to call so late, but we have a minor crisis here. Your granddaughter, the one who won the popularity vote, is in her room crying herself to sleep because she says she has no friends."

Life is sweet and, oh, so short. I once had an old professor who told us that a decision to bring a child into the world was a decision to take out a twenty-year mortgage on your life.

I have found his idea to be true, but his timing was off. That decision is a lifetime mortgage.

You worry and fret with them through their middle school years. Just before all your hair turns gray, just before your stomach does a complete revolution, just before you lose control of all your senses, they grow up.

Too soon they take on a spouse of their own, bring offspring into the world and make you into one of the wisest persons to live since Solomon.

Then, when they call and give you the tearful report of the antics of that complex and perplexing thirteen-year-old, you can smile and think to yourself, "Not my granddaughter. She's the sweetest person I know."